**DIAMOND
PRINTING**

WRITING
RESEARCH
PAPERS

a
complete
guide

JAMES D. LESTER
Austin Peay State University

SCOTT, FORESMAN AND COMPANY
Glenview, Illinois   London

Excerpt from "Hamilton, Alexander" in the *Encyclopaedia Britannica,* © *Encyclopaedia Britannica,* 1967, Vol. 11, published by Encyclopaedia Britannica, Inc., reprinted by permission. Excerpts from *Bibliographic Index, Biography Index, Book Review Digest, Essay and General Literature Index, Reader's Guide to Periodical Literature,* and *Social Sciences and Humanities Index to Periodicals* [formerly *International Index to Periodicals*], reproduced by permission of The H. W. Wilson Company. Excerpt from *Subject Guide to Books in Print, 1966,* reprinted from *Subject Guide to Books in Print, 1966.* Copyright © 1966 by R. R. Bowker Company, 1180 Avenue of the Americas, New York, N.Y. 10036. Excerpt from *Dissertation Abstracts,* Vol. 24, 1963–64, pp. 185 and 1151, reprinted by permission of University Microfilms Library Services. Excerpt from *The New York Times Index,* © 1959 by The New York Times Company, reprinted by permission. Excerpt from *An Index to Book Reviews in the Humanities* (1962) reprinted by permission of Phillip Thomson, Publisher. Excerpt from "Melville's *Billy Budd* as 'An Inside Narrative,'" by William Braswell reprinted from *American Literature,* 29 (May 1957), 138–39, by permission of Duke University Press and the author. Excerpts from Herman Melville's *Billy Budd, Sailor* (*An Inside Narrative*), ed. H. Hayford and M. M. Sealts, Jr., copyright © 1962 by The University of Chicago Press, reprinted by permission of The University of Chicago Press. Excerpt from "Expediency and Absolute Morality in *Billy Budd*" by Wendell Glick, reprinted by permission of the Modern Language Association from *PMLA,* 68 (March 1953), 104. Excerpt from "Among School Children" by W. B. Yeats, reprinted by permission of The Macmillan Company, Mr. M. B. Yeats, and Macmillan & Co. Ltd., from *Collected Poems* by W. B. Yeats. Copyright 1928 by The Macmillan Company, renewed 1956 by Georgie Yeats. Chart from "Cognitive Aspects of Psychomotor Performance" by Edwin A. Locke and Judith F. Bryan, reprinted by permission of the American Psychological Association and Edwin A. Locke. Chart from "Pattern in Language" by Anna H. Live, reprinted from *JGE: The Journal of General Education,* 18 (July 1966), 94, by permission of that journal. Chart from "Stability of the California Short Form Test . . ." by Carmen J. Finley et al., reprinted from the *California Journal of Educational Research* by permission of that journal. Chart from "Toxigenicity of *Clostridium histolyticum*" by Shoki Nishida and M. Imaizumi, reprinted from J. Bacteriology 91:481, 1966 by permission of the American Society for Microbiology.

TABLE OF CONTENTS

PREFACE

In revising this book for a special 1971 printing, I have had two aims: (1) to adhere to the principles of documentation and style set forth by the recently published second edition of the *MLA Style Sheet*, and (2) to provide students with an up-to-date text without undue delay. Accordingly, this Diamond printing of *Writing Research Papers* has been extensively though not wholly altered.

Most sample footnote and bibliography entries have been changed to meet the new guidelines of the *MLA Style Sheet*. The most dramatic change in documentation is the insertion of the name of the publisher in footnote and bibliography entries. Also worthy of note is the use of Arabic rather than Roman numerals designating volume numbers of learned journals (e.g., "32" in place of "XXXII"). Other minor changes also are stipulated, such as special forms for modern reprints and casebooks or the new arrangement of the date for weekly magazines and newspapers (e.g., "21 Nov. 1970" to replace "Nov. 21, 1970").

In certain instances, however, this text offers the instructor and his students a choice of following strictly the *MLA Style Sheet* or of employing a more traditional format. For term papers *MLA Style Sheet* recommends double-spaced quotations, even the long indented ones, and footnotes entirely double-spaced and placed on separate sheets at the end of the work. In contrast, this book maintains the traditional practices of single-spacing long indented quotations and single-spacing footnotes placed at the bottom of each page. Yet this book clearly informs the student that he may be asked to follow strictly the *MLA Style Sheet* guidelines that are explained wherever necessary within the text.

This text differs from the new *MLA Style Sheet* in one additional way. The style sheet stipulates that the year alone (e.g., "1970") is sufficient for the date of a journal article unless the journal's volume number does not coincide with the calendar year, in which case both month and year are necessary (e.g., "November 1970"). However, it seems to this writer that providing both month and year in every instance lessens the chances of error by the student or confusion for the reader, especially in the case of a freshman student reading from an unbound issue of, say, *Modern Fiction Studies* or *PMLA*. Therefore, this text suggests that a student employ both month and year unless he can quickly determine, when using a bound volume, that all issues fall within the same calendar year.

This manual continues to satisfy two additional aims: (1) to tell the beginning researcher everything that he needs to know when he sits down to write a paper: everything from the kind of paper to use, margins, and other mechanical details, to how to choose a topic, organize his paper functionally, and write clear expository prose, and (2) to direct the material to *all* undergraduate students, those in biology, for example, as well as in freshman English.

Equally important, this manual is not a mere mechanical guide to documentation, nor is it a book of rhetoric. Rather, it gives a comprehensive treatment of all problems that face the beginning researcher. For instance, Chapter I tells him how to choose a restricted topic and write a thesis sentence. Next he is shown the mechanics of writing bibliography cards, since he must have this skill before entering the reference room of the library. Thereupon, Chapter III directs him, step by step, to the important reference works in the library. Supplementing this section is a separate appendix (pp. 149–172) that lists reference books and journals separated by disciplines (applied sciences, art, biological sciences, business, and so on).

Thereafter, the student is shown note-taking methods—summary, précis, paraphrase, and direct quotation. Then Chapter V explains the rhetoric of research writing (e.g., outlining, paragraph unity, word choice) and the mechanics of format (e.g., title page, margins, indentation). This chapter also includes a complete specimen research paper. Next, the chapters on footnoting and the bibliography provide over 200 sample entries, including items not often found in research manuals, such as sample entries for source books, modern reprints, and recordings. Chapter VIII, directed toward the science student, shows variations of both the "year and date" system and the "number" system. In addition, it provides 42 sample entries for biology, botany, geology, mathematics, physics, psychology, and zoology.

And to offer instruction that did not fit logically into preceding sections of the manual, I have included a glossary (pp. 139–148) that explains additional research terms not included in the text—that is, everything from accents and Arabic numerals to illustrations. Finally, an exact detailed index quickly directs the student to his desired information.

In conclusion, I wish to extend my thanks to the following persons who made this book possible: my wife, Martha, and sons, Jim and Mark, for their love and patience; Lloyd Lacy, for his research services on this revision; Verne Reaves, for his editorial assistance; Theodore C. Owen and William R. Elkins, for reading the original manuscript; Janice Kramer and Diane Meyer for their contribution to the sample research paper; and numerous members of the faculties of Kansas State Teachers College, the University of Tulsa, and Austin Peay State University.

Clarksville, Tennessee   J.D.L.

THE PRELIMINARIES

Introduction

The research paper is a type of disciplined writing that will enable you to add to your own store of knowledge and to that of others by making an intensive study of a limited topic. It involves collecting and investigating facts and opinions about the topic from numerous sources, and then using them, in an intelligently precise fashion, to provide an answer to some scholarly problem or question.

The topic of a research paper may often be one which, at least initially, you know very little about. At first the task may appear insurmountable: sources to be located, books and articles to be read, note-taking, footnoting of source material, outlining of the paper, writing, rewriting, typing, and proofreading. Perhaps at this point you will begin to question your ability to express yourself in English at all!

Obviously, some kind of orderly process must be applied to the above procedure. This book will help you do that: it outlines the basic research techniques you will need. But of course there is more to writing a good research paper than mere mechanics. Any adequate research assignment asks you to make a definite point, to inform and interest the reader. Once you have found and arranged the material for your paper, you must be able to judge critically the merit of your collected evidence and then be able to arrive at and express demonstrable conclusions about it. Such a task requires concentration and, more importantly, it demands an imaginative molding and adapting of the material. This book will also help you do that: it explains the particular writing style necessary for the presentation of your research findings.

In this respect, it is all too easy to submit a poor manuscript. For example, you might attempt to compile a paper by paraphrasing a few authorities and by inserting quotations abundantly. But such a compilation would prove seriously inadequate since it would merely be presenting commonplace facts and opinions in a research paper format. The thesis of such a paper—if indeed there was one—would not be explored or developed. In other words, you would have offered a recital of investigations without the *commentary* that is the ultimate purpose of all research writing.

To repeat: a research paper asks you to make a point. Here is what one noted scholar has to say about this aspect of the researcher's responsibility to his reader:

> It is our duty because we ought to be kind to our fellow creature; it is [in] our interest because if the view that we wish to put before him is clearly and competently expressed, so that he understands without trouble what we are trying to say, he will be gratified at the smooth working of his own intelligence and will inevitably think better of our theory and of its author than if he had had to puzzle himself over what we mean and then in the end doubt whether his brains are quite what they used to be![1]

In other words, writers of research papers should have the desire and the ability to make a point that will interest and inform the reader.

Research techniques and the ability to shape the material derived from research—these are two of the more important aspects of writing your paper. Along with these, you will also need to acquire a working familiarity with library resources. A college graduate is not expected to know everything; but he should possess the ability to find accurate information about any subject. Self-reliant library research and competent writing will be among your more valuable assets in meeting several kinds of demands: assignments in other courses, reports and studies for business and industry, research articles for publication, and graduate study.

Choosing a Topic

Perhaps the most important advice that can be given you is to select a topic that will be of interest to yourself and to the class. This choice requires more than passing attention; otherwise, you may discover, too late, that your impulsive choice has led you into disappointing results.

In addition, you should observe several other principles in the selection of a topic. First, the topic should be one for which ample reference material is available. Genuine research requires a variety of trustworthy sources. It should demand, therefore, much more than an investigation of one major reference book and one or two encyclopedias. Such limited materials, which will provide a report at most, are not suitable for investigative research. For example, subjects such as "Poetic Meter," "Auto Production in 1970," or "Traffic Death Tolls"

[1] Ronald B. McKerrow, "Form and Matter in the Publication of Research," *Review of English Studies*, 16 (1940), 117.

would not be suitable as research topics because all references would provide almost identical information, and you would have little opportunity for the formulation of judgments.

Next, the topic should be one that has been examined and appraised by critics, experts, and authorities in the field. It should not, therefore, be too new. For example, a news item in this week's newspaper might appear interesting, but research materials would be limited to recent articles, editorials, and columns, providing little depth for development. You should remember, moreover, that the library consists mainly of books and magazines. Accordingly, the subject chosen must be well enough established to have received attention in these works.

A regional topic is permissible if it centers around a region where you live. For example, a student living in Mississippi might choose to write about racial tension in his state. But if you were doing the study of Mississippi while living in Illinois, you would face insurmountable obstacles in gathering materials through interlibrary loans or by expensive travel to Mississippi.

Furthermore, the research paper should usually be nontechnical. A subject that involves technical information is often beyond a beginning writer's ability because of difficult terms and concepts. That is, you should try to avoid topics such as "The Salk Vaccine," "The Xerox Discovery," or "The Apollo Spacecraft" (with this last, the topic is also too recent; the material is, perhaps, classified and unavailable).

Next, the work should be objective in tone. Bias has no place in the research paper. Your thorough examination of all the available evidence should result in responsible, impartial findings. Of course, almost all topics are controversial to some degree; so you should always guard against unsubstantiated personal opinion and prejudice. You might, for example, write about federal aid to education, but careful assimilation and presentation of the evidence would be required to prevent the appearance in your paper of prejudice and unfounded rationalization. Similarly, you would have to use extreme caution in your assessment of findings about such topics as "Protest Demonstrations," "Prayer in Public Schools," or "Urban Renewal."

Other topics to be avoided are: summary, a mere restatement of general material; straight biography, which is usually only summary (though acceptable topics may be developed on the influence of a period of life upon a person or on one aspect of a man's work); sensational topics, such as "The Murder of John F. Kennedy"; a topic that is too broad, such as "The U.S. Presidency"; or one that is not scholarly —there is seldom any place in research writing for such topics as "Fishing for Trout" or "The American Hot Dog."

Finally, you should select a topic that will permit you to form judgments and opinions which you will substantiate and support by authoritative reference material.

In brief, research study demands an evaluation, a formulation of judgments, and a demonstrable conclusion. The topic chosen must offer an opportunity for full development of each of these three points.

Preliminary Reading

You will need a thorough acquaintance with your material before attempting to restrict the subject. Your introductory reading will therefore serve several purposes: it will provide an overview of the subject; it will furnish the beginning of a working bibliography (see pp. 9–14); it will enable you to determine the availability of relevant reference material; and it will make possible a judicious restriction of the subject.

This preliminary reading does not normally require note-taking, since you cannot yet be certain of your needs. As a starting point, you might begin with a book or journal article recommended by your instructor or librarian (see pp. 15–34 for a full discussion of the use and resources of the library). You might also start with a general survey, such as *Literary History of the United States* (see Appendix II, pp. 149–72 for a list of general reference works and journals in your field). Or, you may begin with an encyclopedia, a biographical dictionary, or some other general reference work, as listed below:

ENCYCLOPEDIAS

> *Chambers's Encyclopaedia.* New ed. 15 vols. New York: Oxford Univ. Press, 1959.
> *Collier's Encyclopedia.* 24 vols. New York: Collier, 1965.
> *Columbia Encyclopedia.* 3rd ed. New York: Columbia Univ. Press, 1963.
> *Encyclopaedia Britannica.* 14th ed. 24 vols. Chicago: Encyclopaedia Britannica, 1966.
> *Encyclopedia Americana.* 30 vols. New York: Encyclopedia Americana, 1963.

BIOGRAPHICAL DICTIONARIES
Universal

> **Deceased**
> *Chambers's Biographical Dictionary.* New ed. New York: St. Martin's Press, 1962.
> *Webster's Biographical Dictionary.* 1st ed. Springfield, Mass.: Merriam, 1943.

> **Living**
> *Current Biography.* New York: H. W. Wilson, 1940–date.
> *A Dictionary of Universal Biography ot All Ages and People.* Ed. Albert M. Hyamson. 2nd ed. New York: Dutton, 1951.
> *International Who's Who.* London: Europa Publs. and Allen & Unwin, 1935–date.

Twentieth Century Authors: A Biographical Dictionary of Modern Literature. Ed. Stanley J. Kunitz and Howard Haycraft. New York: H. W. Wilson, 1942. Supplement, 1955.

Webster's Biographical Dictionary. 1st ed. Springfield, Mass.: Merriam, 1943.

World Biography. 5th ed. 2 vols. Bethpage, N.Y.: Institute for Research in Biography, 1954.

American

Deceased

Appleton's Cyclopaedia of American Biography. Ed. J. G. Wilson and John Fiske. 7 vols. New York: Appleton, 1887–1900.

Dictionary of American Biography. 20 vols. New York: Scribner's, 1928–37.

National Cyclopaedia of American Biography. New York: James T. White, 1892-date. (In progress.)

Who Was Who in America. 3 vols. Chicago: A. N. Marquis, 1951–60.

Living

National Cyclopaedia of American Biography. New York: James T. White, 1892-date. (In progress.)

Who's Who in America. Chicago: A. N. Marquis, 1899–date.

Who's Who of American Women. Chicago: A. N. Marquis, 1958–date.

British

Deceased

Dictionary of National Biography. Ed. Leslie Stephen and Sidney Lee. 63 vols. 1885–1901; rpt. in 22 vols., London: Smith Elder, 1908–09. Supplements to 1959.

Who Was Who [1897–1960]. London: Black, 1920–date. (In progress.)

Living

Who's Who. London: Black, 1849–date.

ALMANACS AND YEARBOOKS

The American Yearbook: A Record of Events and Progress. New York: Appleton, 1911–51.

The Americana Annual: An Encyclopedia of Current Events. New York: Americana Corporation, 1923–date.

The Annual Register: A Review of Public Events at Home and Abroad. London: Longmans, Green, 1761–date.

Britannica Book of the Year. Chicago: Encyclopaedia Britannica, 1938–date.

Collier's Year Book. New York: Crowell-Collier, 1939–date.

Facts on File: A Weekly Synopsis of World Events. New York: Facts on File, 1940–date.

Information Please Almanac. New York: Simon & Schuster, 1947–date.

Kane, Joseph N. *Famous First Facts: A Record of First Happenings, Discoveries and Inventions in the United States.* 3rd ed. New York: H. W. Wilson, 1964.

The New International Year Book: A Compendium of the World's Progress, 1907–. New York: Dodd, Mead, 1908–date.

The Statesman's Year-Book: Statistical and Historical Annual of the States of the World, 1864–. London: Macmillan, 1864–date.

The World Almanac and Book of Facts. New York: World-Telegram, 1868–date.

Yearbook of the United Nations. Lake Success, N.Y.: United Nations, 1947–date.

ATLASES AND GAZETTEERS

Adams, James T. *Atlas of American History.* New York: Scribner's, 1943.

Atlas of World History. Ed. R. R. Palmer. Chicago: Rand McNally, 1957.

Bartholomew, John W. *Advanced Atlas of Modern Geography.* 3rd ed. New York: McGraw-Hill, 1956.

Collier's World Atlas and Gazetteer. New York: Collier, 1955.

Columbia-Lippincott Gazetteer of the World. Ed. Leon E. Seltzer. New York: Columbia Univ. Press, 1962.

Encyclopaedia Britannica World Atlas. Chicago: Encyclopaedia Britannica, 1963.

Goode's World Atlas. Ed. Edward B. Espenshade. 12th ed. Chicago: Rand McNally, 1964.

Macmillan World Gazetteer and Geographical Dictionary. Ed. T. C. Collocott and J. O. Thorne. Rev. ed. New York: Macmillan, 1961.

National Geographic Atlas of the World. Ed. M. B. Grosvenor. Washington, D.C.: National Geographic Society, 1963.

Shepherd, W. R. *Historical Atlas.* 9th ed. New York: Barnes & Noble, 1964.

The Times Atlas of the World. Comprehensive ed., produced by *The Times of London* and John Bartholomew & Son. Boston: Houghton Mifflin, 1967.

DICTIONARIES

The American College Dictionary. Rev. ed. New York: Random House, 1967.

Fowler, Henry W., and F. G. Fowler, eds. *The Concise Oxford Dictionary of Current English.* Rev. E. McIntosh. 5th ed. Oxford: Clarendon Press, 1964.

Funk and Wagnalls New Practical Standard Dictionary of the English Language. New York: Funk and Wagnalls, 1964.

Murray, James A. H., et al., eds. *Oxford English Dictionary.* 12 vols. Oxford: Clarendon Press, 1933. Supplement.

Random House Dictionary of the English Language: The Unabridged Edition. Ed. Jess Stein. New York: Random House, 1967.

The Shorter Oxford English Dictionary. Ed. William Little et al. 3rd ed. 2 vols. New York: Oxford Univ. Press, 1962.

Webster's New World Dictionary of the American Language. New York: Meridian Books, 1960.

Webster's Seventh New Collegiate Dictionary. Springfield, Mass.: Merriam, 1963.

Webster's Third New International Dictionary of the English Language. Springfield, Mass.: Merriam, 1961.

Weekley, Ernest. *A Concise Etymological Dictionary of Modern English.* Rev. ed. New York: Dutton, 1952.

BOOKS OF USAGE, SYNONYMS, AND DIALECT

Americanisms: A Dictionary of Selected Americanisms on Historical Principles. Ed. Mitford M. Mathews. Chicago: Univ. of Chicago Press, 1966.

Berrey, Lester V., and Melvin Van den Bark. *The American Thesaurus of Slang.* 2nd ed. New York: Crowell, 1953.

A Dictionary of American English on Historical Principles. Ed. Sir William Craigie and J. R. Hulbert. 4 vols. Chicago: Univ. of Chicago Press, 1936-44.

Fowler, H. W. *A Dictionary of Modern English Usage.* Rev. Sir Ernest Gowers. 2nd ed. Oxford: Clarendon Press, 1965.

Nicholson, Margaret. *Dictionary of American-English Usage: Based on Fowler's Modern English Usage.* New York: Oxford Univ. Press, 1957.

Partridge, Eric. *A Dictionary of Slang and Unconventional English.* 5th ed. New York: Macmillan, 1961.

Perrin, Porter G. *Writer's Guide and Index to English.* Rev. Karl W. Dykema and Wilma R. Ebbitt. 4th ed. Glenview, Ill.: Scott, Foresman, 1968.

Roget's Thesaurus of English Words and Phrases. Rev. Robert A. Dutch. New ed. New York: St. Martin's Press, 1964.
Webster's Dictionary of Synonyms. Springfield, Mass.: Merriam, 1942.
Wentworth, Harold. *American Dialect Dictionary.* New York: Crowell, 1944.

This initial reading need not be extensive since it is intended to provide only a general survey. You will have accomplished your purpose in preliminary reading when you have enough understanding of your material to decide on the restricted phase of it which you wish to pursue.

Restricting the Subject

The effectiveness of a research paper depends mainly upon the support you are able to provide for your judgments and opinions. Detailed treatment of a topic requires you to probe deeply and to present accurate facts and ideas that demonstrate the validity of your contentions. This is one reason why you cannot afford to be too ambitious in what you attempt to cover. Another reason why your topic should be limited to a specific problem or question is that the research paper is a comparatively short work, often no more than about ten typewritten pages in length, excluding title page, outline, and bibliography. The subject should therefore be one that can be handled within these limitations of space, not one that would require twenty or thirty pages for adequate presentation.

Furthermore, you will realize no sense of accomplishment if you present only vague, indefinite statements about a too-extensive, too-generalized subject. For example, most students would not be capable of dealing adequately with "Edgar Allan Poe: His Poetic Genius," but they should get along well with "The Role of the Narrator in 'The Raven.'" Rather than attempting "The American Metropolis," you might write on "The Decline in Unskilled Jobs." And though "The Fur Trade in Frontier America" is probably unmanageable, "A Comparison of the Trapper with the Cowboy as a Frontier Type" might well be within your range.

This restriction of subject requires meticulous study of all available sources. For example, let us say you are assigned the general subject area of the U.S. Presidency. A first step in restriction could be to limit the topic to U.S. Presidents of the twentieth century. Preliminary readings might then suggest a study of one President—John F. Kennedy. You would discover, however, that there is an overwhelming amount of written data about Kennedy. Therefore, you should limit yourself to one aspect of Kennedy's administration—for example, the Cuban missile crisis. At this point you should read the related documents, articles, and books, noting particularly all material about the crisis. You might then decide that Kennedy's major decisions were of utmost importance; therefore, the topic could now read, "Kennedy's Decisions in the Cuban Missile Crisis." Such a restricted topic could probably be handled adequately in an undergraduate paper. You may also discover, of course, that further restriction is possible after note-taking is completed and you are well in command of your material. It is usually only the uninformed, uncertain writer who feels he must take refuge in the "safety" of a large, generalized, unrestricted subject.

Forming a Thesis Sentence

The next great influence upon the success of your work is your ability to limit further the scope of your study with a preliminary thesis sentence. Now that you are progressing more deeply into the subject, you should realize that your completed study will need the unity of a central purpose. Consequently, you should write, in one sentence, a statement of the controlling idea that will unite your various findings. This thesis will thus serve as the nerve center of your paper: it will be amplified and developed with every word, sentence, and paragraph of the study.

The earlier the thesis is formulated, the earlier will a satisfactory working limitation be set on note-taking. However, the thesis sentence may be changed as you progress in the study. You should not bind yourself, early in your work, to a thesis you cannot support or do not believe. In fact, the final, official thesis cannot be properly stated until after note-taking is completed. Nevertheless, a preliminary central idea will aid in the organization of facts, limit the note-taking, and eliminate needless research.

Questions often aid in the discovery of a thesis, but the thesis itself should be a declarative statement. For example, the Kennedy topic above might offer this question: "What motivated Kennedy in his actions and decisions during the Cuban missile crisis?" And such a question might lead to the following thesis statement: "Kennedy's decisions in the Cuban missile crisis reveal his strong determination to protect American interests despite a threat of nuclear war." Clearly, this thesis limits the study to an investigation of Kennedy's interest in the American position, rather than to, say, a detailed examination of Castro's actions, of Khrushchev's decisions, of the naval blockade, or of the arms build-up. In other words, you would now have a workable subject that could be handled within the limitations of space set by the instructor. More significantly, you would have given definite direction to your study.

II

THE WORKING BIBLIOGRAPHY

Early in your study, you should begin the development of a working bibliography. That is, you should begin to compile references which you will eventually investigate as possible source material.

The development of your working bibliography will continue throughout preliminary reading and note-taking. Therefore, during your preliminary reading, you should begin writing bibliography cards for references that you may wish to study later during your note-taking period. In other words, you should watch for footnotes and bibliographies that list new source material. Most books of critical evaluation will contain extensive bibliographies at the end of chapters or at the end of the book. Journal articles usually have footnotes at the bottom of the page and a bibliography at the end of the article. And the general reference works, such as encyclopedias and biographical dictionaries, will normally offer brief bibliographies at the end of each entry.

Suppose, for instance, that your topic concerns some aspect of Alexander Hamilton's political theories. Your preliminary reading of, let us say, *Encyclopaedia Britannica* will uncover not only a brief biography but also the following bibliography:

See also references under "Hamilton, Alexander," in the Index volume.

BIBLIOGRAPHY.—The most satisfactory complete biography, particularly strong on Hamilton's public career, is John C. Miller, *Alexander Hamilton: Portrait in Paradox* (1959). The most scholarly study is Broadus Mitchell, *Alexander Hamilton*, 2 vols. (1957, 1962). Nathan Schachner, *Alexander Hamilton* (1946) is a short, well-balanced and readable study. For an extended essay on Hamilton's economic and political ideas, see Louis M. Hacker, *Alexander Hamilton in the American Tradition* (1957); for careful selections of Hamilton's writings on various subjects interspersed with editorial comment, see Richard B. Morris, ed., *Alexander Hamilton and the Founding of the Nation* (1957); Broadus Mitchell, *Heritage From Hamilton* (1957); and Saul K. Padover, ed., *The Mind of Alexander Hamilton* (1958). Publication of a multi-volume work, *The Papers of Alexander Hamilton*, edited by H. C. Syrett and J. E. Cooke, began in 1961. See also David Loth, *Alexander Hamilton: Portrait of a Prodigy* (1939); Henry Jones Ford, *Alexander Hamilton* (1920); Allan M. Hamilton, *The Intimate Life of Alexander Hamilton* (1910); Frederick S. Oliver, *Alexander Hamilton: an Essay on American Union* (1906); Gertrude Atherton's interesting novel on Hamilton, *The Conqueror* (1902); William Graham Sumner, *Alexander Hamilton* (1890); Henry Cabot Lodge, *Alexander Hamilton* (1882); John T. Morse, Jr., *The Life of Alexander Hamilton*, 2 vol. (1876); and the works of Hamilton's son, John C. Hamilton, *The Life of Alexander Hamilton*, 2 vol., (1840–41), an unfinished biography that goes only to 1787, and his valuable but uncritical *History of the Republic of the United States of America, as Traced in the Writings of Alexander Hamilton*, 7 vol., 3rd ed. (1868).   (A. DE C.)

HAMILTON, ANTHONY (*c.* 1645–1719), French writer,

Fig. 1: From *Encyclopaedia Britannica*

Since several of these sources will appear promising, you will want to begin making bibliography cards, such as:

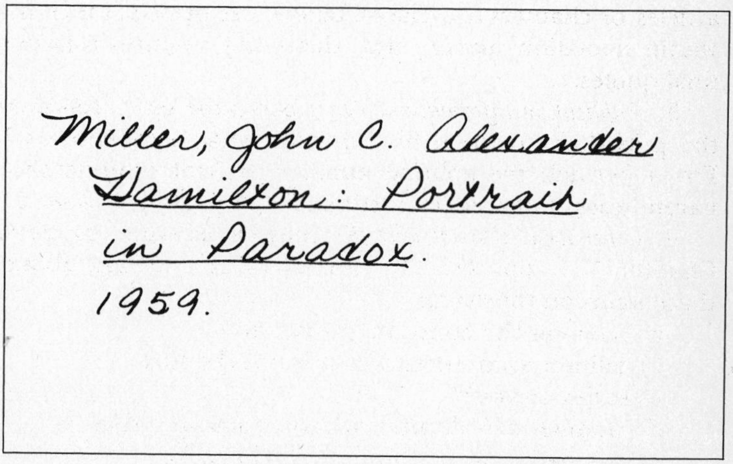

Fig. 2: Sample Bibliography Card

> *Miller, John C. Alexander Hamilton: Portrait in Paradox.*
>
> *1959.*

Later, at the card catalog, you can insert the proper library call number (see pp. 27–31), the place, and the publisher. Then, when you are ready to study this particular book, your card provides the information for finding it. In addition, this card contains the necessary data for your final bibliography.

A word of caution, however. You should recognize that adding to the bibliography during preliminary reading and during note-taking is only incidental to your main bibliographical development. After preliminary reading and your selection of a restricted topic, you will need to investigate thoroughly all avenues of approach to the subject. To that end, you should follow the procedures set forth in Chapter III, "The Library" (pp. 15–34), which directs you to the important bibliographies and indexes in your library's reference room. In these books you will discover a vast array of source material. Your stack of bibliography cards will grow rapidly, providing a valuable index to the range and scope of past and recent scholarship related to your subject.

As you discover each new reference, you should record the bibliographical data onto *individual* cards. (Normally, 3 x 5 cards are used; for taking notes, 4 x 6 note cards are usual.) You should also check carefully to make certain that each bibliography card includes the following:

1. *Author's name*, followed by a period. Arrange the name in inverted order, surname first, for alphabetizing purposes. Provide the name in

the fullest form available, e.g., "Hart, Tom P.," not "Hart, T. P."

2. *Title of the work.* Underline titles of books, journals, magazines, and newspapers. Spell in full titles of periodicals. Titles of books are followed by a period; titles of periodicals by a comma. Titles of articles or chapters are placed before the principal title and are placed within quotation marks; also, this entry requires a period inside the final quotes.

3. *Publication information.* For a book: the place, followed by a colon; the publisher, followed by a comma; the date, followed by a period. For a journal: the volume number in Arabic numerals; the date in parentheses, followed by a comma; the page(s), followed by a period.

4. *Other items of documentation* may be necessary, as shown below (see Chapter VII, pp. 117–30, for exact information about positioning these items on the card):

    a) name of the editor or translator
    b) edition used, whenever it is not the first
    c) series number
    d) number of volumes with this particular title
    e) volume number if one of two or more

5. *Library call number* of a book or magazine, placed in the upper right-hand corner of the card. This item is valuable when the material is actually needed.

6. *A personal note,* at the bottom of the card, as to the type of material to be found in this source or any special aspect it presents.

Specimen Bibliography Cards

In addition to the examples provided below, you may also study the bibliographical entries in Chapter VII:

Fig. 3: Card for an Entire Book

Fig. 4: Card for an Entire Book

821.91
Au2Z s2

Spears, Monroe K. *The Poetry of W. H. Auden*. New York: Oxford Univ. Press, 1963.

Contains critical discussion of Auden.

Fig. 5: Card for a Section of a Book

810.8
M 617ap

Miller, Perry, ed. *The American Puritans: Their Prose and Poetry*. Garden City, N. Y.: Doubleday, 1956.

Has comments on Thomas Shepard, 143-44.

Fig. 6: Card for Introduction to a Book

320
L 66 Le

Rossiter, Clinton, and James Lare, eds. "Introduction." *The Essential Lippmann*. New York: Random House, 1963.

Check introduction for comments on Lippmann.

320
L66 Ze

Lippmann, Walter. "The Public and the People." _The Essential Lippmann_. Ed. Clinton Rossiter and James Lare. New York: Random House, 1963. Defines "the people" on 85-87.

Fig. 7: Card for a Section of a Book

973
H25
V. 15

MacDonald, William. _Jacksonian Democracy, 1829-1837_. In _The American Nation: A History_. Ed. Albert B. Hart. 28 vols. New York: Harper, 1906. XV, 43-66.

Fig. 8: Card for One Volume of Several

Churchill, Henry Stern. "United Nations Headquarters — a Description and Appraisal." _Architectural Record_, 112 (July 1952), 104-22. On function and purpose of buildings.

Fig. 9: Card for a Periodical Article

Fig. 10: Card for a
Periodical Article

> Gleckner, Robert F. "William
> Blake and the Human
> Abstract." *PMLA*, 76,
> No. 4, Pt. 1 (Sept. 1961),
> 373-79.
>
> Treats "The Divine Image"
> and "A Divine Image."

Fig. 11: Card for a
Periodical Article

> Pearsall, Robert Brainard.
> "The Presiding Tropes of
> Emily Brontë." *College
> English*, 27 (Jan. 1966),
> 267-73.
> Inspects figurative quality
> of her prose to emphasize
> her poetic qualities.

Fig. 12: Card for a
Casebook Refer-
ence

> Brooks, Cleanth. "*The Waste
> Land*: Critique of the Myth."
> *Modern Poetry and the
> Tradition*. Chapel Hill:
> Univ. of North Carolina
> Press, 1939. Rpt. in *Storm
> Over the Waste Land*. Ed.
> Robert E. Knoll. Chicago:
> Scott, Foresman, 1964.

III

THE LIBRARY

Now that you have an overview of your subject together with a restricted topic, a thesis sentence, and the beginning of your working bibliography, you need a system of library study that will save time and labor. This chapter suggests a step-by-step method of investigation that should produce thorough coverage of your topic: it takes you first to the bibliographies and indexes, then to the card catalog, and finally to the books and articles themselves. Following this system will ensure efficiency and skill in the preparation of your paper.

Before beginning formal research, you may wish to tour the library to learn its organization. Your tour should include the information desk, the reference room, the card catalog, the periodicals room, and the stacks (if they are open to students).

The Information Desk

Here you may receive a booklet or chart that outlines the arrangement of the library or you may discuss its facilities with a librarian. In either case, you should acquaint yourself with the special services of the library: interlibrary loans, special collections, microfilm and viewing machines, the availability of typewriters and photocopying machines, audio-visual aids, and so on.

The Reference Room

An experienced researcher usually begins his investigation in the reference room. There he gathers a list of sources from bibliographies, indexes, and other works of reference. Later, at the card catalog, he supplements his list and records call numbers. Only then does he begin serious reading for note-taking.

You may employ this same procedure. Already you should have a few bibliography cards that you recorded during your preliminary reading in encyclopedias and other general works. You should now expand this small list into a full working bibliography by consulting the bibliographies and indexes in the reference room of your library. Keep in mind, however, that these works do not provide information for note-taking. But they do list other works where you will find detailed treatment of your topic. They direct you to books, pamphlets, and articles in collections, magazines, and newspapers. Also, some indexes specialize in one type of source (for example, *Readers' Guide to Periodical Literature* indexes magazines only). Other indexes specialize in one field (for example, *Education Index, Bibliography of American Literature,* and *Dramatic Bibliography*).

A word of caution, however. Bibliographies and indexes classify their listings according to individual systems that vary from work to work. Before using any index, you should study its preliminary pages to determine its system of abbreviations, symbols, and classification. And, since indexes appear weekly, bi-monthly, monthly, and yearly, you should look closely at the date of publication of each one you select. For example, if your topic concerns a contemporary problem, you would probably want to start your investigation with the most recent listings.

Because reference works must serve many students, you must not take them from the library. Rather, you should read them in the reference room, leaving them on the table so that the librarians may return them to their proper position on the shelves.

BIBLIOGRAPHIES

You will find bibliographies published separately or within such other works as encyclopedias, general reference books, critical and biographical studies, and scholarly journals. Also, you will note two types: standard bibliographies, which list sources in existence for some time, and current bibliographies, which list recent publications.

As a beginning researcher, you need a comprehensive listing of reference materials in your subject field. To that end, Appendix II of this manual contains lists of reference works and journals in the following subject areas: applied sciences (pp. 149–52), art (152–54), biological sciences (pp. 154–56), business (pp. 156–57), education (p. 157), English language and literature (pp. 157–60), foreign languages (pp. 160–61), health and physical education (pp. 162–63), home economics (p. 163), music (pp. 163–65), philosophy (p. 165), psychology (pp. 165–66), religion (pp. 166–67), social sciences (pp. 167–71), and speech and drama (pp. 171–72).

In addition you will find thorough coverage of your field in any of the following sources—that is, each of these books functions as a bibliography that offers a list of other bibliographies:[1]

Barton, Mary N., comp. *Reference Books: A Brief Guide for Students and Other Users of the Library*. 6th ed. Baltimore: Enoch Pratt Free Library, 1966.

Murphey, Robert W. *How and Where to Look It Up*. New York: McGraw-Hill, 1958.

Shores, Louis. *Basic Reference Sources: An Introduction to Materials and Methods*. Chicago: American Library Association, 1954.

Walford, Arthur J., ed. *Guide to Reference Material*. London: Library Association, 1959. Supplement, 1963.

Winchell, Constance M. *Guide to Reference Books*. 8th ed. Chicago: American Library Association, 1967. Supplements, 1965–66 and 1967–68.

Let's assume you wish to proceed with the investigation of Alexander Hamilton begun in the previous chapter. You would first examine the listings under "History" in Appendix II of this manual (p. 169) or in one of the books listed above. As a result, you would find such works as:

American Historical Association. *Guide to Historical Literature*. Ed. George F. Howe and others. New York: Macmillan, 1961.

Beers, Henry Putney. *Bibliographies in American History: Guide to Materials for Research*. Rev. ed. New York: H. W. Wilson, 1942.

Handlin, Oscar, and others, eds. *Harvard Guide to American History*. Cambridge, Mass.: Belknap Press, 1954.

Examining these under the appropriate heading, you would then search for special bibliographies of Hamilton, such as:

Ford, Paul Leicester. *Bibliotheca Hamiltoniana: A List of Books Written by, or Relating to Alexander Hamilton*. New York: Knickerbocker Press, 1886.

This discovery would narrow the search to a "subject" bibliography —that is, one that treats one topic exclusively.

In addition to special bibliographies, you should also examine:

Bibliographic Index: A Cumulative Bibliography of Bibliographies. New York: H. W. Wilson, 1938–date.

Although *Bibliographic Index* originally covered only the years 1937–42, it is kept current by supplements. It is therefore valuable for bringing your investigation of a topic up-to-date. (Note, for instance, that the publication date for the Hamilton bibliography by P. L. Ford was 1886. You can thus see that the need often arises for more

---

[1] A work of international scope is Theodore Besterman, *A World Bibliography of Bibliographies*, 4th ed., 5 vols. (Lausanne: Societas Bibliographica, 1965).

current material.) Sample entries from *Bibliographic Index* and a supplement follow:

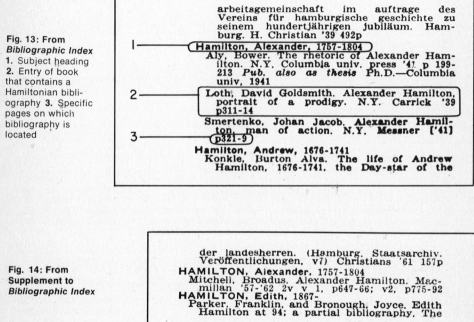

Fig. 13: From
Bibliographic Index
1. Subject heading
2. Entry of book
that contains a
Hamiltonian bibli-
ography **3.** Specific
pages on which
bibliography is
located

Fig. 14: From
Supplement to
Bibliographic Index

You will note that each entry in *Bibliographic Index* directs you to the specific bibliographic section within a critical study. In other words, by consulting this text, you would have discovered not only the four books about Hamilton but also four additional bibliographic lists. For example, a bibliography on Alexander Hamilton will be found in Broadus Mitchell's *Alexander Hamilton,* published by Macmillan in 1957 and 1962, on pages 647–66 of volume 1 and pages 775–92 of volume 2.

Another reference aid of this general nature is *Bulletin of Bibliography and Magazine Notes* (Boston: F. W. Faxon, 1897–date). The first page of each volume contains an index.

TRADE BIBLIOGRAPHIES

You may also have occasion to use the trade bibliographies, which are works intended primarily for use by booksellers and librarians. You will find them helpful in three ways: to discover sources which may not be listed in other bibliographies or in the card catalog of your library; to locate facts of publication, such as place and date; and to learn if a book is in print.

Certainly, you should become familiar with *Books in Print* (New York: Bowker, 1948 – date). This work provides an author-title index to the *Publishers' Trade List Annual* (New York: Bowker, 1874 – date), a list of books currently in print. Also, *Publishers' Weekly* (New York: Bowker, 1872 – date) offers current publication data. In addition, *Subject Guide to Books in Print* (New York: Bowker, 1957 – date) supplies a subject index that enables you to discover new sources. For example, the 1966 edition contains the following entry:

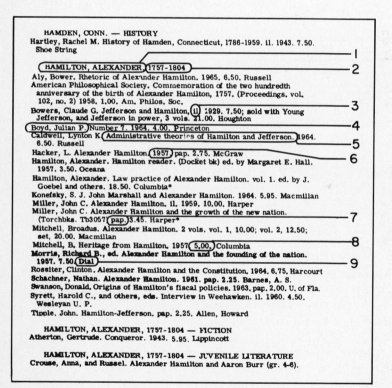

Fig. 15: From *Subject Guide to Books in Print* 1. Subject 2. Dates of subject's life span 3. Book contains illustrations 4. Author 5. Title 6. Date of publication 7. Paperback book 8. Price 9. Publisher

In short, you cannot overlook the trade bibliographies. Others are:

Paperbound Books in Print. New York: Bowker, 1955 – date.
Since the publication of paperback books is increasing annually and

since important books are occasionally found *only* in paperback form, you may find this text a necessary tool.

Cumulative Book Index. Minneapolis [later New York]: H. W. Wilson, 1900 – date.
> This work lists books by author, subject, editor, and translator. Use it to find complete publication data or to locate *all* material in English on a particular subject.

The National Union Catalog: A Cumulative Author List. Ann Arbor, Mich: Edwards, 1953 – date.
> Basically, this work is the card catalog in book form; that is, it provides a list representing the Library of Congress printed cards and also titles reported by other libraries. It supplements the *Library of Congress Catalog.*

Library of Congress Catalog: Books: Subjects, 1969. Washington, D. C.: Library of Congress, 1970.
> This catalog complements *The National Union Catalog* by supplying a subject classification. Separate volumes are available for the years 1950 – 54, 1955 – 59, 1960 – 64, and annually thereafter.

General Catalogue of Printed Books. London: Trustees of the British Museum, 1881 – date.
> This British publication serves a corresponding function to *The National Union Catalog.* Such listings are available for most nations.

Union List of Serials in Libraries of the United States and Canada. 3rd ed. New York: H. W. Wilson, 1965. Supplements, *New Serial Titles*, Washington, D. C.: Library of Congress, 1953 – date.
> You may consult this work to determine if a nearby library has a magazine that is unavailable in your library.

Ulrich's Periodical Directory. Ed. Eileen C. Graves. 12th ed. 2 vols. New York: Bowker, 1967-68.
> This work is a guide to current periodicals, both domestic and foreign.

INDEXES

A general index furnishes the page number(s) of another book or magazine where you will find specific information. Fundamentally, there are three types: indexes to materials in books and collections, indexes to literature in periodicals, and indexes to materials in newspapers.

Indexes to Books and Collections

First, you should recall *Bibliographic Index* (see pp. 17 – 18), which also refers you to books or collections. In addition, you should be familiar with:

> *Essay and General Literature Index, 1900 – 1933.* Comp. Minnie E. Sears and Marian Shaw. New York: H. W. Wilson, 1934. Supplements, 1934 – date.
> *Biography Index: A Cumulative Index to Biographical Material in Books and Magazines.* New York: H. W. Wilson, 1946/47 – date.

The first index directs you to material of a biographical and/or critical nature. Note the following entry from the 1960 – 64 supplement:

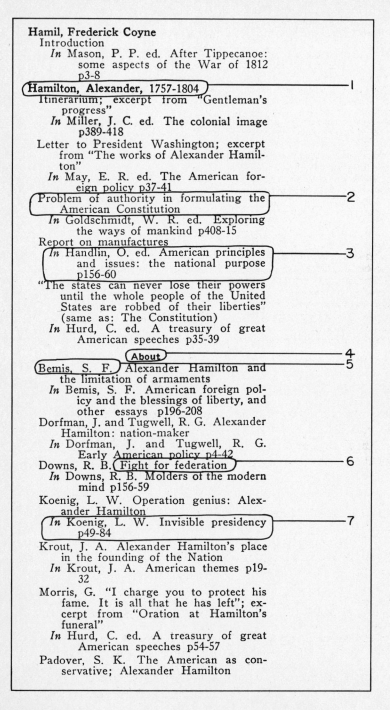

Hamil, Frederick Coyne
Introduction
  In Mason, P. P. ed. After Tippecanoe:
    some aspects of the War of 1812
    p3-8
Hamilton, Alexander, 1757-1804 — 1
Itinerarium; excerpt from "Gentleman's
    progress"
  In Miller, J. C. ed. The colonial image
    p389-418
Letter to President Washington; excerpt
    from "The works of Alexander Hamil-
    ton"
  In May, E. R. ed. The American for-
    eign policy p37-41
Problem of authority in formulating the — 2
    American Constitution
  In Goldschmidt, W. R. ed. Exploring
    the ways of mankind p408-15
Report on manufactures
  In Handlin, O. ed. American principles — 3
    and issues: the national purpose
    p156-60
"The states can never lose their powers
    until the whole people of the United
    States are robbed of their liberties"
    (same as: The Constitution)
  In Hurd, C. ed. A treasury of great
    American speeches p35-39
    About — 4
Bemis, S. F. Alexander Hamilton and — 5
    the limitation of armaments
  In Bemis, S. F. American foreign pol-
    icy and the blessings of liberty, and
    other essays p196-208
Dorfman, J. and Tugwell, R. G. Alexander
    Hamilton: nation-maker
  In Dorfman, J. and Tugwell, R. G.
    Early American policy p4-42
Downs, R. B. Fight for federation — 6
  In Downs, R. B. Molders of the modern
    mind p156-59
Koenig, L. W. Operation genius: Alex-
    ander Hamilton
  In Koenig, L. W. Invisible presidency — 7
    p49-84
Krout, J. A. Alexander Hamilton's place
    in the founding of the Nation
  In Krout, J. A. American themes p19-
    32
Morris, G. "I charge you to protect his
    fame. It is all that he has left"; ex-
    cerpt from "Oration at Hamilton's
    funeral"
  In Hurd, C. ed. A treasury of great
    American speeches p54-57
Padover, S. K. The American as con-
    servative; Alexander Hamilton

Fig. 16: From *Essay and General Literature Index*
1. Subject **2.** Article by Hamilton **3.** Book in which Hamilton's essay appears **4.** Designates that following essays are *about* Hamilton, rather than essays written *by* him **5.** Author of essay about Hamilton **6.** Title of the essay **7.** Book in which the essay appears

As shown above, the *Essay and General Literature Index* lists writings *by* the author as well as essays *about* him. In addition, you should note, for example, that L. W. Koenig's "Operation Genius: Alexander Hamilton" will be found in L. W. Koenig's *Invisible Presidency*, published by Rinehart in 1960, on pages 49–84 (the publisher and date are found in a "List of Books Indexed" at the end of each volume of *Essay and General Literature Index*).

On the other hand, *Biography Index* is a good starting point if your study involves a famous person. It gives clues to biographical information for people of all lands. (However, for the years 1900–47 you should see *Essay and General Literature Index.*) Note the following excerpt from *Biography Index:*

Fig. 17: From *Biography Index* 1. Subject 2. Dates of subject's birth and death 3. Subject's profession 4. Authors of the biography 5. Title of the biography 6. Publisher (in this instance, a magazine) 7. Volume and page numbers (volume 91, pp. 93ff) 8. Portrait 9. Date of publication (March 1964) 10. Contains a bibliography 11. Illustrated

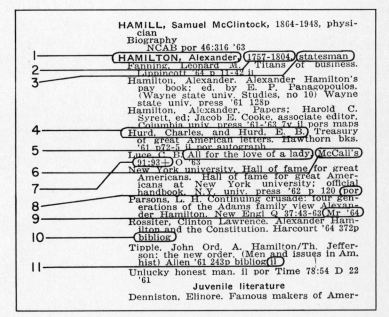

Most indexes published by the H. W. Wilson Company use this same code system. Specifically, note the code for journal volumes and page numbers—"37:43–63." To conform to the suggestions in this manual, you will want to record this data differently on your bibliography card, as follows:

Parsons, L. H. "Continuing
Crusade: Four Generations
of the Adams Family
View Alexander Hamilton."
New England Quarterly,
37 (March 1964), 43-63.

When looking for biographical information, you should also consult a good biographical dictionary (see pp. 4–5).

Another important index is the cumulated subject and author indexes to *Dissertation Abstracts International* (Ann Arbor, Mich.: University Microfilms, 1970). (Formerly *Microfilm Abstracts*, 1938–51, and *Dissertation Abstracts*, 1952–69.) Issue number 12, part II, of each volume contains the cumulated subject and author indexes for issues 1 through 12 in the volume's two sections—A, Humanities and Social Sciences, and B, Sciences and Engineering. For example, the subject index of volume 24, No. 12, Part II, offers the following:

HAMBURG—POLITICS AND GOVERNMENT

The politics of labor in Hamburg, 1918-192٦. ·
R. A. Comfort.   **XXIV**, 3310

HAMILTON, ALEXANDER, 1757-1804

Alexander Hamilton and the British orientation
of American foreign policy, 1783-1803. H. V.
Johnson.   **XXIV**, 1151

HAMMETT EQUATION

The application of the Hammett equation to the
benzyl system. D. M. Carlton. **XXIV**, 3975

**Fig. 19: From the
Index to *Dissertation Abstracts***

This entry directs you to page 1151 of Volume 24 of *Dissertation Abstracts* where you will find an abstract of a dissertation by Helene Vivan Johnson. A portion of that abstract follows:

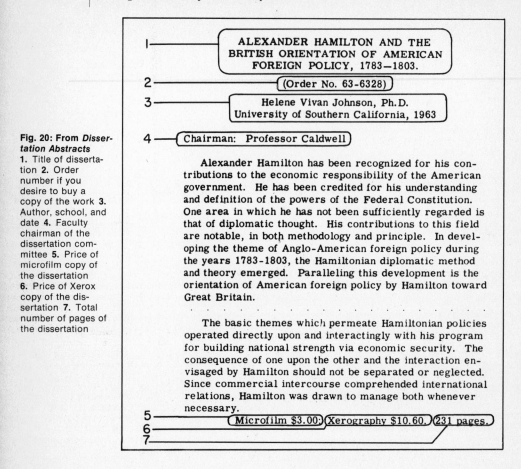

Fig. 20: From *Dissertation Abstracts*
1. Title of dissertation 2. Order number if you desire to buy a copy of the work 3. Author, school, and date 4. Faculty chairman of the dissertation committee 5. Price of microfilm copy of the dissertation 6. Price of Xerox copy of the dissertation 7. Total number of pages of the dissertation

1 ——— ALEXANDER HAMILTON AND THE BRITISH ORIENTATION OF AMERICAN FOREIGN POLICY, 1783–1803.

2 ——— (Order No. 63-6328)

3 ——— Helene Vivan Johnson, Ph.D. University of Southern California, 1963

4 ——— Chairman: Professor Caldwell

Alexander Hamilton has been recognized for his contributions to the economic responsibility of the American government. He has been credited for his understanding and definition of the powers of the Federal Constitution. One area in which he has not been sufficiently regarded is that of diplomatic thought. His contributions to this field are notable, in both methodology and principle. In developing the theme of Anglo-American foreign policy during the years 1783-1803, the Hamiltonian diplomatic method and theory emerged. Paralleling this development is the orientation of American foreign policy by Hamilton toward Great Britain.

. . . .

The basic themes which permeate Hamiltonian policies operated directly upon and interactingly with his program for building national strength via economic security. The consequence of one upon the other and the interaction envisaged by Hamilton should not be separated or neglected. Since commercial intercourse comprehended international relations, Hamilton was drawn to manage both whenever necessary.

5 ——— Microfilm $3.00; Xerography $10.60. 231 pages.
6 ———
7 ———

The abstract, of course, is only a brief summary of the entire work. If the dissertation is pertinent to your topic or if you plan an exhaustive investigation, you may wish to order a copy of the complete work from University Microfilms, Inc., Ann Arbor, Michigan. To that end, information at the end of the abstract stipulates the cost of microfilm and Xerox copies of the complete dissertation.

Indexes to Literature in Periodicals

Because they provide four types of information better than any other source, you must use articles in periodicals. Understandably, they contain: the most recent materials on any subject; obscure, temporary, or extremely new materials; the climate of opinion of a particular period; and supplements to professional literature. For example, materials often appear as journal articles before their publication in book form.

There are two main types of periodicals: general periodicals (for example, *Time, Look,* or *Ladies Home Journal*); and professional journals (for example, *National Tax Journal, Mathematical Review,* or *Journal of Psychology*). You will use both types, of course, but you should depend mainly upon the learned journals whose treatment of topics is more critically detailed.

As an index to articles in periodicals, you should first investigate:

Readers' Guide to Periodical Literature. New York: H. W. Wilson, 1900–date.

A sample entry follows:

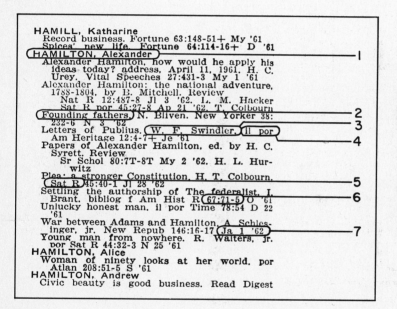

Fig. 21: From *Readers' Guide to Periodical Literature* 1. Subject **2.** Title of article **3.** Author **4.** Illustrated with a portrait **5.** Name of magazine **6.** Volume and page numbers (volume 67, pp. 71–75) **7.** Date (January 1, 1962)

In most instances, this index directs you to general periodicals, though from 1953 on scientific periodicals have been included. If you wish to examine the scholarly journals, such as *New England Quarterly* and *Political Science Quarterly*, you should investigate:

Social Sciences and Humanities Index [1907–date; formerly titled *International Index to Periodicals*]. New York: H. W. Wilson, 1916–date.

A sample entry from *Social Sciences and Humanities Index* follows:

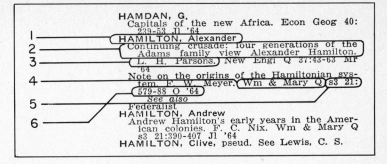

Fig. 22: From
Social Sciences
and Humanities
Index 1. Subject
2. Title of article
3. Author 4. Name
of journal 5. Series
and volume num-
ber 6. Page num-
bers and date

Next, you should investigate:

> *Nineteenth Century Readers' Guide to Periodical Literature, 1890–1899*
> [with supplementary indexing, 1900–22]. 2 vols. New York: H. W. Wil-
> son, 1944.

> *Poole's Index to Periodical Literature, 1802–1881.* Rev. ed. Boston:
> Houghton Mifflin, 1891. Supplements cover the years 1882–1906.
>> With this work you may locate information on materials from 1802–
>> 1906. Note that *Poole's Index* has only a subject classification. See,
>> however, Marion V. Bell and Jean C. Bacon, *Poole's Index Date and
>> Volume Key* (Chicago: Association of College and Reference Li-
>> braries, 1957) for an alphabetical title listing.

Newspaper Indexes

Newspapers are an excellent source of information. Therefore, you
should familiarize yourself with the *New York Times Index* (New York:
New York Times, 1913–date). It indexes not only the *New York Times*
but also indirectly indexes most other newspapers by revealing the date
on which the same news was probably reported in other newspapers.
Many libraries have the *New York Times* on microfilm. A sample entry
from the *New York Times Index* follows:

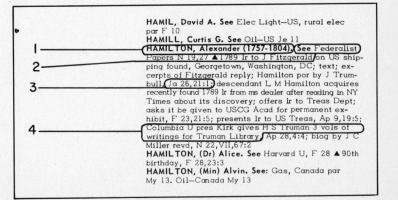

Fig. 23: From *New*
York Times Index
1. Subject **2.** Cross
reference **3.** Date,
page number, and
column number
(January 26, p. 21,
column 1) **4.** Title
of newspaper
article

For example, the last entry on Hamilton in the *New York Times Index* is a review of J. C. Miller's biography of Hamilton which appears in the *New York Times,* November 22, Part VII, page 67, column 2 (sections of the Sunday edition are shown by a Roman numeral).

For British newspapers a similar index is *Official Index* [to *The London Times*] (London: Times, 1907–date). It is available in most American libraries.

Pamphlet Indexes

The principal index to most pamphlet material is:

Vertical File Index: A Subject and Title Index to Selected Pamphlet Material. New York: H. W. Wilson, 1932/35–date.

Your library may not own many of the items listed, but the catalog gives a description of each entry, the price, and the means by which you may purchase it.

Finding the Call Number

After completing your work in the reference room, you should turn next to the card catalog, which specifies the location of all books in the library. (Most libraries have a separate, smaller catalog for periodicals.) With your bibliography cards arranged alphabetically, you can easily find and record the call number for each book. If, after exerting sufficient effort, you cannot locate a catalog card, you may seek help from a librarian.

For each book you will usually find in the catalog three separate entries (or more), filed under: (1) the author's name, printed on the first line (see p. 28); (2) the title of the work, typed in black ink at the top of the card (see p. 28); and (3) the subject, typed in red ink at the top of the card (see p. 31). Additional catalog cards are filed for coauthors, translators, editors, and illustrators, and for other subject headings.

MAIN ENTRY CARD

As you go through the card catalog you will quickly discover that there is a main entry card for each book you are seeking, usually filed under the author's name. For example:

Fig. 24: Main Entry Card (Author Card) 1. Classification number **2.** Author number **3.** Author **4.** Birth date of author **5.** Title **6.** Edition **7.** Place of publication **8.** Date of publication **9.** Publisher **10.** Technical description: size, number of pages, illustrations, etc. **11.** Note on contents of book

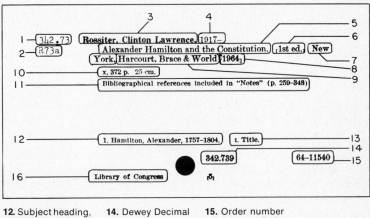

12. Subject heading, card filed under subject's name **13.** Subject heading, card filed under title of the work

14. Dewey Decimal System number

15. Order number — Library of Congress **16.** Publisher of this card

You may gather several kinds of information from this main entry card. Specifically, you should record the *complete* call number — in this case, $\frac{342.73}{R73a}$. Do not copy the first line only! You must have the full number, usually consisting of two (and sometimes three) lines of symbols. In addition, you should record any bibliographical notations, such as "Bibliographical references included in 'Notes' (p. 259–348)." Data of this sort can direct you to additional sources.

TITLE CARD

Another card is always filed alphabetically by the book title:

Fig. 25: Title Card 1. Title, usually typed in black ink **2.** Main entry card filed under "Hamilton, Alexander" **3.** Editor (see below, item 5) **4.** Subject headings (see Subject card, p. 31) **5.** Separate card filed under name of editor **6.** As we see, a card is filed by the title of the work **7.** Library of Congress number

A third type of card found in the catalog is the subject card—but we will come to that in a moment.

THE CALL NUMBER

The library classifies and arranges its books by the call number, which is usually a combination of the Dewey Decimal System and the Cutter Author Number. In a call number such as $\frac{330.973}{\text{H18p}}$, the first line is the Dewey Decimal Number, and the second line is the Cutter Author Number. The Dewey system divides all books into ten general classifications:

000–099	General Works
100–199	Philosophy
200–299	Religion
300–399	Social Sciences
400–499	Language
500–599	Pure Science
600–699	Technology (Applied Sciences)
700–799	The Arts
800–899	Literature
900–999	History

The Dewey system then divides each of these ten general classes into ten smaller divisions. For example, the general literature classification (800–899) is broken down into:

800–809	General Works [on Literature]
810–819	American Literature
820–829	English Literature
830–839	German Literature
840–849	French Literature
850–859	Italian Literature
860–869	Spanish Literature
870–879	Latin Literature
880–889	Greek and Classical Literature
890–899	Literature of Other Languages

Next, American Literature (810–819) is divided into the following classifications:

811	Poetry
812	Drama

813   Fiction
814   Essays
815   Speeches
816   Letters
817   Satire and Humor
818   Miscellany
819   Minor Related Literature

Further subdivisions of each of these groups separate the works of literature until a specific number is designated for each book (for example, 814.21 or 816.143).

Immediately below the Dewey classification number, most libraries also insert an author number, a set of letters and numerals based on the Cutter Three-Figure Author Table. For example, "H18p" is the author number for Alexander Hamilton, *Papers on Public Credit, Commerce and Finance.* The letter "H" is the initial of the author's last name; next, the Cutter table stipulates the Arabic numeral "18"; and finally, the lower case "p" designates the first important letter in the title to distinguish this entry from other writings by Hamilton. Thus, the complete call number for Hamilton's book is $\frac{330.973}{\text{H18p}}$. You must employ both items to locate the book.

Some libraries employ the Library of Congress classification system, which features capital letters followed by Arabic numerals to designate the subdivisions (for example, JK154 for *The Federalist* or E302.6 for Broadus Mitchell's *Alexander Hamilton*). The major divisions of the Library of Congress system follow:

A   General Works and Polygraphy
B   Philosophy and Religion
C   History and Auxiliary Sciences
D   History and Topography
     (excluding America)
E-F America
G   Geography and Anthropology
H   Social Sciences
J   Political Science
K   Law
L   Education
M Music
N   Fine Arts
P   Language and Literature
Q   Science

R Medicine
S Agriculture and Plant and Animal Husbandry
T Technology
U Military Science
V Naval Science
Z Bibliography and Library Science

Using the Catalog as an Index

The card catalog indexes all important subject areas by means of subject cards and tabular headings. This is the third kind of card to be found in the catalog. For example, if your subject is Public Debts, you would discover under "Debts, public" an index to all books in the library on this subject. Note the following subject card:

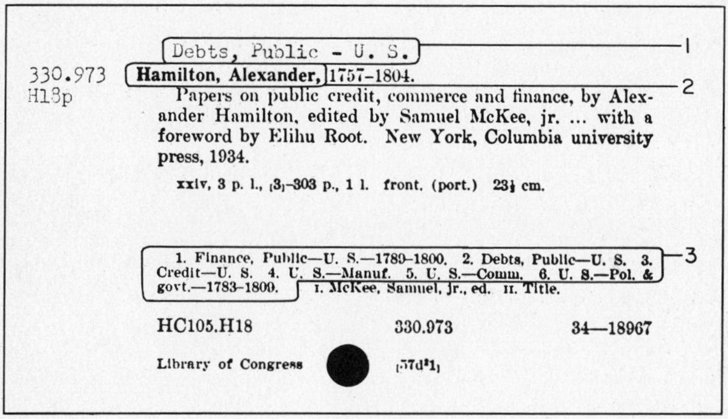

Debts, Public - U. S. — 1

330.973 Hamilton, Alexander, 1757-1804. — 2
H18p

Papers on public credit, commerce and finance, by Alexander Hamilton, edited by Samuel McKee, jr. ... with a foreword by Elihu Root. New York, Columbia university press, 1934.

xxiv, 3 p. l., [3]-303 p., 1 l. front. (port.) 23½ cm.

1. Finance, Public—U. S.—1789-1800. 2. Debts, Public—U. S. 3. Credit—U. S. 4. U. S.—Manuf. 5. U. S.—Comm. 6. U. S.—Pol. & govt.—1783-1809. I. McKee, Samuel, jr., ed. II. Title. — 3

HC105.H18 330.973 34—18967

Library of Congress [37d²1]

Fig. 26: Subject Card (See also "Main Entry Card," p. 28, and "Title Card," p. 28) **1.** Subject heading, usually typed in red ink **2.** Main entry card filed under "Hamilton, Alexander" **3.** Other subject headings under which you will find this same card (see below)

The library makes a subject card of this nature for every topic developed within each book. As shown above, the library will index this same book by Hamilton under these other subject headings:

Finance, Public – U.S. – 1789 – 1800
Credit – U.S.
U.S. – Manuf.
U.S. – Comm.
U.S. – Pol. & govt. – 1783 – 1809

In other words, the card catalog of your library is, among other things, a subject index to the books it lists.

Other Catalog Cards

Temporary cards are of a different color and usually indicate that a book is not in circulation. However, ask the librarian about the book, for it may be available:

Fig. 27: Temporary Card

```
                                                    4-5-66

        66-384   Hamilton, Alexander
                 The works of Alexander Hamilton
                 . . . 1904.


                 Gen
                 12 v.


                  BOOK ON ORDER
                        ◯
```

Cross-reference cards refer you to alternate or related headings. There are two types. The "see" card indicates the correct heading under which material is listed:

Fig. 28: Cross-Reference Card

```
        U. S.-History-Reconstruction
            see
        Reconstruction




                        ◯
```

The "see also" card directs you to related subjects that contain additional material:

```
Reconstruction
  see also
Southern States—History—1865—
```

Fig. 29: "See Also" Card

In short, your best procedure with the card catalog is a combination of practices: you can easily record call numbers while you search for new sources. For example, with your bibliography cards in hand, you should look first under the proper subject heading—"Hamilton," in this instance. There you will find index cards for all books *by* Hamilton and most books *about* him. At the same time, you will discover the call numbers for the majority of your sources. In addition, you may uncover new sources that supplement your working bibliography.

Getting Your Books and Periodical Articles

THE STACKS

Armed with the correct call numbers, you are now ready to locate your books in the stacks or, in the case of closed stacks, to request the books from a clerk. If a book is unavailable, you may request a "hold" on the book. When it returns, the librarian will reserve it for you.

THE RESERVE DESK

Recognizing the importance of certain books to their disciplines, many instructors place them "on reserve" in the library so that a limited number of books will be available to many students. You will want to determine if any books necessary for your research are on reserve. To that end, you should ask the clerk at the desk to explain the filing system employed.

If you use a reserve book, you must usually read it in the library. Some libraries, however, permit overnight withdrawal of reserve books. But under no circumstances should you keep such a book for several days or hide it somewhere in the library for future use. These books must serve many students.

THE PERIODICALS ROOM

You will locate periodical articles in both bound and unbound volumes. The bound ones, usually on open stacks, contain several issues within a hard cover. The unbound volumes are usually of recent publication. If periodicals are kept in closed stacks, you must provide the clerk with sufficient publication data.

Supplementing Library Materials

Without doubt the library is your best source of information when writing a research paper. But you may also find material in other places. For instance, you could write your U.S. Senator or Congressman for one of the many booklets printed by the Government Printing Office. You will find a list of these materials, many of which are free, in a monthly catalog issued by the Superintendent of Documents, *United States Government Publications Monthly Catalog* (Washington, D. C.: GPO, 1895 – date).

Also important are audio-visual materials: films, filmstrips, music, phonograph recordings, slides, and tape recordings. You may find these in the library or in some other location on or off campus.

Other good sources of information are: radio and television programs, lectures, letters, public addresses, personal interviews, and questionnaires.

IV

NOTE-TAKING

After the completion of your preliminary investigation, you may direct your note-taking toward the solution or clarification of one specific problem. By this time you should have completed preliminary readings, having gained in this an initial familiarity with the range of your sources. Also, you should have framed a thesis sentence for your restricted topic, determining thereby the specific direction you will pursue in your study. In addition, you should have in hand the beginning of your working bibliography, to which you will add new references as you come upon them during the process of note-taking.

The Preliminary Outline

A well-written outline will help you ensure paragraph coherence and stylistic unity. To achieve the desired outline, you should follow several progressive steps: (1) jot down your ideas in a rough list; (2) organize a preliminary outline by categorizing your list of ideas; and (3) expand the development of your preliminary outline into a formal topic or sentence outline (see pp. 50–53 for a discussion of outline forms). In order for your selection and paraphrasing of material to contribute exactly to the scheme of your paper, you should complete items (1) and (2) before you begin taking notes. In other words, now is the time to prepare a preliminary outline. This preliminary outline should be based upon ideas that you absorbed while choosing and restricting your subject and while forming your thesis sentence or purpose statement.

Suppose, for example, that you read Herman Melville's novella *Billy Budd* and that you wrote the following purpose statement for your paper:

> The purpose of this paper is to examine Melville's use of biblical references in <u>Billy</u> <u>Budd.</u>

Your intentions are clear: you will examine the biblical references, searching, meanwhile, for Melville's purpose in using them. As a first step, you should list your supporting ideas in random order, as in the following:

```
Billy Budd = Adam
Billy's innocence
Claggart is evil = Satan?
Billy's fall from grace
David and Saul
Joseph and his brothers
Good and Evil
Abraham and Isaac
Vere as Abraham?
Billy as Isaac?
Are the characters symbolic?
The Bible treats good and evil
What would Vere symbolize?
```

Obviously, this list is not an outline, but you now have your ideas on paper where you may examine them and find relationships. You should now organize the items, grouping your main topics and relating subordinate elements to them. Thus, you will divide your ideas into separate categories that will, in turn, suggest the structure of your research paper. And, since you may separate your material in various ways, you should consider a few methods of organization and classification.

First, select an overall plan of procedure, either general to particular (deductive) or particular to general (inductive). If you arrange your materials deductively, you will present first a general statement that you will afterwards support with specific details and instances. For example, you might wish to state a generalization first: "President Nixon's continued escalation of the Vietnam war was necessary." You could then show that specific, successive events proved him correct. Similarly, you could use the general to particular scheme in other research papers: to state the theme of an author and to prove it with details from his writings; to present the conclusions of a laboratory experiment and to state the particulars; or to declare the dishonesty of a dictator and then to present your proof. In other papers, however, you may wish to use the particular to general order. Using this technique, you would reverse the above process and, writing inductively, present first the specifics of your argument and then work carefully toward a general conclusion.

After selecting one of the two external orders, you should consider your internal arrangement, that is, the way in which you will classify and present the various factors of your argument. Having selected, for

example, a general to particular arrangement for the Vietnam topic
mentioned above, you would open with a generalization, perhaps to the
effect that President Nixon's added escalation into Cambodia was necessary for the control of Communist aggression in Southeast Asia. You
could then order your supporting material by using one or more of
the methods listed below.

CAUSE AND EFFECT

You may employ cause and effect, listing, for example, reasons for
President Nixon's various assumptions and decisions and/or the effects
of them. In this way, you would examine the reasons why something
is true or you would study the result of some action or idea. The cause
and effect method of classification is effective for examining social
issues, such as civil rights, school prayers, or extremist groups, and for
exploring such topics as a musician's style, a biological experiment, or a
pattern of psychological behavior.

COMPARISON AND CONTRAST

After examining your Vietnam topic, you might choose one of
the following plans: (1) a comparison and/or contrast of President
Nixon's assumptions with those of Senator J. W. Fulbright; (2) a comparison and/or contrast of the Vietnam war with the Korean War;
or (3) a comparison and/or contrast of the Pentagon "hawks" with the
Senate "doves." In short, you could discuss your subject in relation to
another subject. In other research papers, you might compare and/or
contrast two works by an artist or a poet, compare and/or contrast
the political climate of one state with that of another state, or compare
and/or contrast the results of two similar experiments.

SPATIAL ORDER

Spatial order is the backbone of descriptive writing. Your focus of
attention moves logically from one detail to another as you describe, for
example, political regions, geographic or topographic features of the
land, or the design of a city, housing development, flower, chair, and so
on. The Vietnam topic would require a spatial order if you examined
the strategic location of Vietnam in relation to its neighbors.

CHRONOLOGICAL ORDER

With the Vietnam topic you may wish to show, chronologically,
that specific, successive events have proved Nixon correct. Therefore,

you would present your particulars in the order of their happening. With other research papers you could trace chronologically a literary theme through several works of an author, arrange your historical study by time sequence, or show the step-by-step method of a laboratory process. However, because you must reach judgments and conclusions about the events, you will seldom use pure narration or storytelling in writing the average research paper. In other words, even though you discuss a series of happenings, you will probably use other methods, such as cause and effect or comparison and contrast.

COMBINING THE METHODS OF ARRANGEMENT

Several of the methods of ordering your outline just discussed may be used at the same time. For example, you could arrange your Vietnam paper chronologically with three events: the sending of advisers to Vietnam, the troop build-up, and the Vietnamization program. However, since you must also reach certain judgments within each of the three time divisions, you would probably also employ cause and effect as a subdivision, listing the causes of certain events and the resulting effects. Similarly, the "Billy Budd" preliminary outline (see below — the complete "Billy Budd" paper is on pp. 80–96) shows the writer utilizing the particular to general order by listing instances that point toward Melville's general purpose. Within each section of that outline, the writer should obviously resort to the comparison and contrast method. And he must, if he is to be successful, discuss the effect of each comparison upon Melville's general purpose. Obviously, he cannot escape an overlapping of methods. Neither can you, but if you select carefully an external plan and an internal one, the subdivisions should logically follow. (See pp. 50–64 for an additional discussion of rhetorical methods.)

ARRANGING YOUR LIST OF IDEAS

Looking again at the list of ideas above (p. 36) for the "Billy Budd" paper, you can see that the biblical allusions will form the core of the sample preliminary outline. This preliminary outline might appear as follows:

```
   I.   Good and evil--the Bible and Billy Budd
  II.   Billy and Adam
 III.   David and Saul--Billy and Claggart
  IV.   Joseph and his brothers
   V.   Abraham and Isaac
  VI.   Characters symbolize good = Billy
                           evil = Claggart
                              ? = Vere
```

Brief as it is, such an outline as this one will help you locate and record the important, necessary data and omit information that looks valuable but that, in fact, contributes little to your overall plan. The outline is ragged and incomplete, but only you will see it. Such a preliminary outline represents roughly the best you can do before note-taking.

Moreover, you should not feel bound to this first outline. Instead, let it develop and grow; add new topics and discard others, rearrange your order, evaluate topics, and subordinate minor elements. In short, as your ideas materialize, you should allow your outline to expand accordingly. (Before writing your final outline, however, see pp. 50–53.)

Examining Your Source Material

You need not, of course, read everything, but you should skim all potentially relevant material to determine its relationship to your thesis and rough outline. Upon discovery of pertinent information, you can then write accurate, detailed notes. But again, you should record only that material which will aid the development and clarification of your thesis.

Also, you should closely examine each book to see if it contains, in addition to its text, any of the following: a table of contents, preface, introduction, index, glossary, appendix, footnotes, or bibliography. By reading a table of contents, for example, you might discover that only one chapter of a book treats your topic. An author's preface may explain the presence or absence of certain material. An introduction will include a critical overview of the book. The index of a book will help you discover whether the book discusses your subject at all. Equally important, a glossary lists and defines terms, an appendix offers additional material, and the bibliography and footnotes suggest new sources.

Finally, you should utilize the most recent, reliable sources of information. Since you are expected, always, to form sound judgments based on the merit of your collected evidence, you should closely evaluate outdated or biased material. In this regard, note that most critics discuss the judgments and opinions of other authorities. Thus, if your source refers to a certain writer as a recognized authority, a good check would be to record this fact and then carefully inspect that writer's work. When in doubt about the validity of a source, you may counsel with your instructor or consult the *Book Review Digest* (New York: H. W. Wilson, 1905–date). A sample entry from a recent volume of *Book Review Digest* follows:

Fig. 30: From *Book Review Digest* **1.** Author, title, and facts of publication **2.** Call number and subject entry for card catalog **3.** Reviewer's description of the book **4.** Reviewed favorably by the reviewer **5.** Reviewed both favorably and unfavorably by the reviewer **6.** Reviewer's judgment of the book **7.** Facts of publication of the review—*New York Times Book Review* (April 15, 1962), p. 16 **8.** Number of words in the complete review

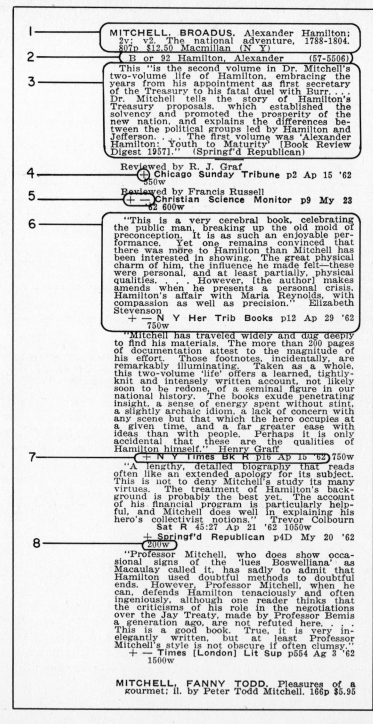

Arranged alphabetically by author, the *Book Review Digest* provides an evaluation of several thousand books each year.

Additionally, you could examine the *Index to Book Reviews in the Humanities* (Detroit: Phillip Thomson, 1960–date). A sample entry follows:

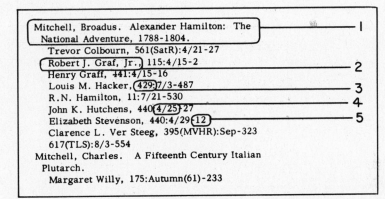

Fig. 31: From *Index to Book Reviews in the Humanities* **1.** Author and title of book **2.** Name of reviewer **3.** Magazine or book number (a numbered list at the front of each volume of the index gives the name of the magazine or book in which the review is found) **4.** Date **5.** Page number

And you will find additional evaluation of source material in any of the following:

The Booklist. Chicago: American Library Association, 1905–date.
> This work offers a selective list of new books that will meet the needs of the average public library. Annotations make it valuable for student usage.

The Reader's Adviser. Rev. and enl. by Hester R. Hoffman. 11th ed. New York: Bowker, 1968.
> This work provides a systematic treatment of many books, as indicated by its subtitle: "a guide to the best in print in literature, biographies, dictionaries, encyclopedias, bibles, classics, drama, poetry, fiction, science, philosophy, travel, history."

United States Quarterly Book List. New Brunswick. N. J.: Rutgers Univ. Press, 1945–56.
> Critical annotations and biographies of the authors make this a valuable reference. However, you will not find recent material because it has ceased publication.

Using Primary and Secondary Sources

Whenever possible, you should make use of primary sources—that is, the original works of an author. Primary sources include novels, short stories, poems, letters, diaries, notes, manuscripts, documents, and autobiographies. Remember, an author's own words are often the most valid source of information for both direct quotation and paraphrase.

On the other hand, you should also make extensive use of articles about the subject by various authorities. These secondary sources include articles found in learned journals and book-length critical studies. However, in reading these sources, you must judge carefully the difference between fact and opinion. Just because a statement is in print does not validate it. You must learn to rely primarily on facts, and then base your own interpretations and opinions upon these. Still, if certain opinions or interpretations seem valuable to the discussion, you might wish to include them in the notes, though clearly labeled as opinion. In your later readings, perhaps, you will discover other authorities lending credence to an opinion. The weight of such evidence would then authenticate what, at first, seemed opinion.

Technique of Note Cards

As with the bibliography cards, you should be exact in recording note card information. The following system may prove helpful:

1. Write the notes legibly in ink — penciled notes become blurred because of repeated shuffling of the cards.

2. In general, use 4 x 6 cards for taking notes. The larger card distinguishes the notes from the 3 x 5 bibliography cards and provides more adequate space for writing the note.

3. Place only *one* item of information on each card. You may then shuffle and rearrange the cards during all stages of organization.

4. Since material on the back of a card may be overlooked, write on only one side of the card. However, if material should run a few lines beyond the one side on occasion, finish it on the back. But in such a situation, write "OVER" conspicuously on the face of the card.

5. Before writing the note, indicate in an abbreviated form the source of the information. Use a brief form, inasmuch as full information on the reference is available on the bibliography card. The identification may be the title of the book, the name of the author, or both. (Some students prefer a key number system, which involves numbering each bibliography entry. When a particular reference is used, this key number is then placed on the card. The danger of this technique, however, is the possibility of losing the key.)

6. Always place the proper page number at the top of each note card, since the bibliography card will not contain this specific page reference needed for a footnote entry.

7. Also, label the note card to indicate the kind of information it contains. This label at the top of the card will speed arrangement of notes with the outline.

8. Finally, write the note, using one of four basic methods: summary, précis, paraphrase, or quotation. (See below for a discussion of each method.)

Methods of Note-Taking

SUMMARY

You should write a summary note card only when the source material is of doubtful or limited importance. In other words, you probably will not use the material; yet it may somehow prove helpful later in the study. You should write, therefore, a brief sketch of the material, without great concern for style or expression. Summaries will usually lack the neatness of the other forms, although you should still take care that you make proper interpretation of the authority. Your chief purpose with the summary, as well as with the précis (see pp. 44–45) and paraphrase (see pp. 45–46), is to extract all significant facts. You must devote, at this time, sufficient energy to this task; otherwise, it will still remain to be done if you take the easy way and unthinkingly copy entire paragraphs verbatim. Also, you should remember that the summary requires a footnote when placed in the text. A sample note card follows:

```
Theme of B.B.                Weaver, pp. 37-38




Fall of Billy like fall of man--both show
God's glory. Melv. wrote B.B. to express his
faith: "evil is defeat" & "natural goodness
invincible."
```

Fig. 32: Summary Note Card

Provided below is the material from which this note was drawn:

Just as some theologians have presented the fall of man as evidence of the great glory of God, in similar manner Melville studies the evil in Claggart in vindication of the innocence of Billy Budd. For, primarily, Melville wrote *Billy Budd* in witness to his ultimate faith that evil is defeat and natural goodness invincible in the affections of man.[1]

[1]Raymond Weaver, "Introduction," *The Shorter Novels of Herman Melville* (1928; rpt. New York: Premier-Fawcett, 1960), pp. 37–38.

PRÉCIS

The précis is a very brief summary in your own words, differing from the rough summary in being more polished in style and differing from the paraphrase in being more concise. You should write the précis in complete sentences in formal English. (Only the rough summary allows abbreviations and sentence fragments.) Moreover, you must make certain that the précis is accurate in context and connotation. That is, you should preserve the essential truth of the reference material. Consequently, you will have success with the précis if you:

1. Condense the original with precision and directness. Reduce a long paragraph into a few sentences, tighten an article into a paragraph, and summarize a longer work, such as a biography, into a few pages.

2. Preserve the tone of the original. If the original is humorous, for example, maintain that tone in the précis. In the same way, retain moods of satire, exaggeration, doubt, irony, and so on.

3. Limit the use of key words or phrases from the original, and write the précis in your own language. However, retain exceptional words and phrases from the original, enclosing them in quotation marks.

4. Provide a footnote locating the source of your material.

A sample précis note card follows:

Fig. 33: Précis Note Card

```
        Vere's nature          Braswell, AL, 138-39




              Centering their attention on Vere, critics
        view him either sympathetically as a man con-
        scientiously doing his duty or disapprovingly
        as a "monstrous villain" who enforces unjust
        laws that violate personal freedoms.
```

Provided below is the material from which this note was drawn:

Before going into more detail about the symbolism, however, it is necessary to analyze the role of Captain Vere, because on whatever plane one reads the novel, he is the key figure. The good-hearted Billy Budd and the evil Claggart have inspired relatively little dissent among critics: one is as inescapably good as the other is inescapably evil. The crux of the problem is what to make of their commanding officer, who alone sees and understands the situation, and yet, knowing Billy to be essentially innocent, summarily has him hanged for striking the blow that accidentally kills the master-at-arms. Most criticism of the novel treats Vere sympathetically, as a conscientious man who does his duty as he sees it. But some of the later criticism pictures him as a monstrous villain—a depraved martinet who enforces iron-clad laws regardless of whether they violate individual rights. He is charged with overweening personal ambition, hypocrisy, and the abuse of confidence.[1]

PARAPHRASE

You will probably write most of your notes in the form of paraphrase. In this type of note, you restate, in your own style, the thought or meaning expressed by another. In other words, you borrow an idea, opinion, interpretation, or statement of an authority and rewrite it in your own language. Furthermore, you write the note in about the same number of words as the original, hence the distinction between paraphrase and précis, the latter being a very *brief* summary.

Obviously, you should choose only important materials for such treatment. Material of doubtful importance should be summarized, while bulky references should be condensed with a précis. Furthermore, it is generally wiser to paraphrase material rather than to indiscriminately fill card after card with directly quoted matter. One danger of relying primarily on quoted materials is that they may lead you into plagiarism (see pp. 47–49). Of course, you are saved from plagiarism in the use of paraphrase only if you credit the thoughts you have borrowed by means of a footnote. The point of view and the presentation may be yours, but the idea, you must always remember, belongs to the original author. A sample paraphrase note card follows:

```
Vere compared with Pontius Pilate
              E. L. Grant Watson, NEQ, 323




    E.L. Grant Watson finds a parallel between
Captain Vere and Pontius Pilate because both
men condemn known innocents. However, Watson
praises Vere for accepting "full responsibility"
for his judgment and the consequent "bitter-
ness," unlike Pilate who washed his hands of
the execution of Jesus.
```

Fig. 34: Paraphrase Note Card

[1] William Braswell, "Melville's *Billy Budd* as 'An Inside Narrative,'" *American Literature*, 29 (May 1957), 138–39.

Provided below is the material from which this note was drawn:

> In Captain Vere we find a figure which may interestingly be compared to Pontius Pilate. Like Pilate, he condemns the just man to a shameful death, knowing him to be innocent, but, unlike Pilate, he does not wash his hands, but manfully assumes the full responsibility, and in such a way as to take the half, if not more than the half, of the bitterness of the execution upon himself.[1]

QUOTATION

Students frequently overuse direct quotation in taking notes, and as a result they overuse quotations in the final paper. Probably only about ten per cent of your final manuscript should appear as directly quoted matter. Therefore, you should strive, in note-taking, to limit the amount of exact transcribing of source materials. The point of research writing is to make yourself a master of your subject matter; the overuse of quotations indicates that you are not sure of yourself in this respect and are using quotations as a crutch to provide substance, or perhaps only as padding. Originality in research writing requires a personal presentation of thoroughly assimilated material. Accordingly, it should be you speaking in the major portion of your paper, giving, of course, proper credit where credit is due. You should reserve direct quotations for material that is the best evidence on the subject, that is said with especially brilliant clarity, or that is subject to refutation.

In addition, you should place quotation marks around material that is directly quoted on the note cards to distinguish it from paraphrases and the like. When thus quoting, you should copy the exact words of the author, even to the retention of any errors in the original (see "sic," p. 116). A sample note, quoting a primary source, follows:

```
Billy's nature                          Melville, 86




          ". . . he had none of that intuitive knowledge
          of the bad which in natures not good or incom-
          pletely so foreruns experience, and there-
          fore may pertain, as in some instances it
          too clearly does pertain, even to youth."
```

Fig. 35: Quotation Note Card[2]

---

[1] E. L. Grant Watson, "Melville's Testament of Acceptance," *New England Quarterly*, 6 (June 1933), 323.

[2] Herman Melville, *Billy Budd, Sailor (An Inside Narrative)*, ed. Harrison Hayford and Merton M. Sealts, Jr. (Chicago: Univ. of Chicago Press, 1962), p. 86.

A sample note card, quoting a secondary source, follows:

```
Vere's nature                W. Y. Tindall, 73-74



"Captain Vere is faced with a dilemma.
Though he believes in Billy's innocence, naval
law and prudence alike demand punishment for
the impetuous seaman while pity and reason
counsel mercy."
```

Fig. 36: Quotation Note Card[1]

Avoiding Plagiarism

A student often unintentionally misuses his sources. Others may do so intentionally. But since you will be working with the writings of others, it is important that you learn and follow certain ethical rules as to the use of reference material. Fundamentally, plagiarism is the offering of the words or ideas of another person as one's own. Of course, the most flagrant violation is appropriating the exact words of another and offering them without documentation. But the theft is often much more subtle. The following list will suggest several forms of research writing that will constitute, in the eyes of all instructors, plagiarism:

1. The use of another's writing without proper use of quotation marks. Do not, under any circumstances, copy onto your paper a direct quotation without providing quotation marks and without crediting the source.

2. The borrowing of a phrase, the use of an idea, or the paraphrasing of material if that phrase, idea, or material is not properly introduced and documented. Also included in this category of plagiarism is the mere rearrangement of phrases from the original into a new pattern.

3. The use of another student's work. (Obviously!)

Another author's ideas, interpretations, and words are his property;

[1]William York Tindall, "The Ceremony of Innocence," in *Great Moral Dilemmas in Literature, Past and Present,* ed. Robert M. McIver (New York: Harper & Row, 1956), pp. 73-74.

they must be acknowledged as such. Consequently, you should practice the following rules of conduct when using the material of others:

1. Acknowledge borrowed material within the text by introducing the quotation or paraphrase with the name of the authority from whom it was taken.

2. Enclose within quotation marks all quoted materials.

3. Make certain that paraphrased material is written in your own style and language. The simple rearrangement of sentence patterns is unacceptable.

4. Provide a footnote for each borrowed item.

5. Provide a bibliography entry for every book or magazine that appears in the footnotes.

The examples provided below should reveal to you the difference between genuine research writing and plagiarism. First, here is an example of original reference material; it is followed by three student versions, only one of which would *not* be called plagiarism:

Original Material

> *Wuthering Heights* is the most remarkable novel in English. It is perfect, and perfect in the rarest way: it is the complete bodying forth of an intensely individual apprehension of the nature of man and life. That is to say, the content is strange enough, indeed baffling enough, while the artistic expression of it is flawless.[1]

Student Version A

```
        The most remarkable novel in English is
Wuthering Heights.  It brings forth an  indi-
vidual apprehension of the nature of man and
life; therefore it is perfect in the rarest
way.  The artistic expression is flawless, but
the content is strange, indeed baffling.
```

This piece of writing is plagiarism in its most deplorable form. The student has simply reversed the order of each sentence, retaining the essential phrasing. He provides no documentation whatever, which implies to the reader that these sentences are entirely his original creation.

---

[1]Walter Allen, *The English Novel* (New York: Dutton, 1954), p. 223.

Student Version B

> Wuthering Heights is a great English
> novel. It is perfect in the rarest way: it
> provides an individual apprehension of man's
> nature. The artistic expression is flawless,
> although the content is strange and baffling.[1]
>
> [1]Walter Allen, The English Novel (New
> York: Dutton, 1954), p. 223.

This student's version is also plagiarism, even though he carefully documents the citation. He has obviously copied almost directly from his source, changing only a few words and phrases. His method is neither summary nor paraphrase. This error may be avoided by direct quotation or, preferably, by a scholarly paraphrase that may include some direct quotation of any strikingly significant or well-worded ideas.

Student Version C

> Walter Allen insists that the "artistic
> expression" of Wuthering Heights is flawless.[1]
> Allen admits that the content is strange and
> even baffling, but he argues that the novel is
> perfect because it accurately presents "an in-
> tensely individual apprehension of the nature
> of man and life."[2]
>
> [1]Walter Allen, The English Novel (New
> York: Dutton, 1954), p. 223.
>
> [2]Ibid.

This version represents a satisfactory handling of the source material. The authority being cited is identified and acknowledged at the outset, the substance of his comment is well expressed in the student's own language, and a key idea in the original, one strikingly worded, is directly quoted, so as to give full credit where the credit is due. The student has been wholly honest to his source, and he has made effective use of the authority for his own purposes.

V

WRITING YOUR PAPER

During the course of research, you have been making judgments and comparisons and putting details into order and completing them. You are now ready to synthesize all research materials into a paper that will give the greatest possible clarity, orderliness, and meaning to your findings. But before beginning the actual writing, you should first formulate a detailed, exact outline.

The Outline

Your rough outline should now be expanded into a clear, logical plan that will guide your paragraph development. Remember, however, that you are not bound by your original plan. If you see possibilities in a new arrangement, you should, by all means, try it.

Since you will write your final outline for your instructor and other readers, you should follow recognized conventions. First, use the standard outline symbols:

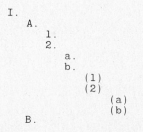

And so on. Your indentation of each heading will indicate the importance of the material; that is, you will progress from major concepts to minor ones. The degree to which you continue the subheads will depend, in part, upon the complexity of your subject; but, as a general rule, you should seldom find it necessary to carry the subheads beyond the first series of small letters.

In addition, headings of like rank on the same margin should have an equal importance. And, if you establish equal ideas, give them parallel form. Note the following:

```
I. Spring sports
   A. To play baseball
   B. Tennis
   C. Track
```

Obviously, the infinitive phrase "To play baseball" is not parallel with the nouns "Tennis" and "Track." If A is a noun, then make B and C nouns also, or if you prefer, make them all infinitives; but do not mix the grammatical forms.

When you indent outline headings, you are subordinating your ideas. Thus, if you find yourself attempting to enter a single subhead, you obviously have one major idea and not several subordinate ones. Note the following:

```
I. Spring sports
   A. Baseball
      1. History
   B. Tennis
      1. History
   C. Track
      1. History
```

Clearly, the writer intends to discuss the history of the sports. Therefore, he might rearrange the entries in the following manner:

```
Spring Sports

 I. The History of Baseball
    A. Origin
    B. Growth
    C. Maturity
II. The History of Tennis
```

Since a reader knows that your introduction is first and that the conclusion is last, you need not insert such labels into your outline. Instead, you should name specifically the contents of that section (see sample outlines, pp. 52, 82–83).

Because it is the main idea of the entire paper and no other idea can rank equally with it, you should not label your thesis sentence as item I in the outline. Otherwise, you may find yourself searching fruitlessly for a parallel idea to put in II, III and IV. Instead, you should write your thesis sentence separately, placing it above the outline proper.

You may write your outline in topic, sentence, or paragraph form, remembering, of course, that you cannot alternate forms within a given outline. With the topic outline, every heading is a noun or its equivalent, a gerund phrase or an infinitive phrase. With the sentence outline, every heading is a sentence or the major headings are nouns and the subheads sentences. With the paragraph outline, every heading is a paragraph or the major headings are nouns and the subheads are paragraphs; however, you will seldom use the paragraph outline, although it is valuable for papers that require multiple, complex details.

Reproduced below is a portion of the "Billy Budd" outline (see pp. 82–83 for the complete topic outline) in topic, sentence, and paragraph form:

Topic Outline

    Thesis sentence: Melville uses biblical references to support his interpretation of the moral issues that govern men's lives.

  I. The Bible and <u>Billy</u> <u>Budd</u>
    A. The Bible
      1. Righteousness
      2. Wickedness
    B. <u>Billy</u> <u>Budd</u>
      1. A story of man's fall
      2. A gospel story
    C. Biblical references
      1. Characters, ideas, and symbols
      2. Moral issues
        a. Ambiguities
        b. Rights and duties
 II. Billy Budd and Adam

Sentence Outline

  I. The Bible and <u>Billy</u> <u>Budd</u>
    A. The Bible clarifies good and evil.
      1. It praises righteousness.
      2. It condemns wickedness.
    B. Like the Bible, <u>Billy</u> <u>Budd</u> explores the realm of good and evil.
      1. Melville centers his story around the fall of man.
      2. He also writes a type of gospel story.
    C. Melville intentionally uses biblical references.
      1. He presents characters, ideas, and symbols.
      2. He thereby offers moral principles that govern our lives.
        a. He shows the ambiguities of these principles.
        b. He pictures both the rights and obligations of man.
 II. Billy Budd and Adam

Paragraph Outline

  I. The Bible and <u>Billy</u> <u>Budd</u>
    A. For centuries the Bible has clarified both good and evil. Its characters portray success and failure, righteousness and wickedness.
    B. <u>Billy</u> <u>Budd</u> possesses many characteristics of the Bible. Newton Arvin says that Melville bases the story on the fall of man, and Raymond Weaver calls it a gospel story.
    C. Intentionally using his biblical references, Melville distinguishes characters, ideas, and symbols. In this way, he presents the moral principles that

```
         govern our lives.  E. L. Grant Watson insists that
         Melville wishes to show the ambiguities of good and
         evil.  Certainly, the reader discovers both man's
         struggle between good and evil and the complexity of
         man's rights and duties.
   II. Billy Budd and Adam
```

Preparing to Write

If you begin writing your paper at least one full week before it is due, you should have sufficient time for writing, revising, and re-writing. However, you should not rush into the writing; instead, you should (1) examine your thesis sentence and outline to see that they provide you with a well-rounded, logically organized plan of procedure; (2) examine your tone to see that it suits your topic, purpose, and audience; and (3) examine your note cards to see that support for your ideas is abundantly supplied.

Ask yourself, "Do I know my main idea and supporting ideas?" If in doubt, you must read your thesis sentence and your outline again. With an objective eye you should examine your ideas and their logical progression through the outline. At this point you cannot afford ambiguity because each of your paragraphs must develop and expand your thesis sentence.

Next ask yourself, "Do I know my purpose?" To answer this question, you must consider both the intellectual framework (what you want the reader to understand) and the emotional framework (what you feel and what you want the reader to feel). Thus, you will have to present your material from a selected perspective that will influence your handling of the subject and your audience's reaction to it.

For example, suppose your topic deals with extremist violence in our streets. Obviously, you face an intellectual choice: you may defend or condemn the extremist groups. Complete objectivity is unlikely in a research paper which is, in fact, a form of argument. Moreover, you will determine your emotional framework by assuming either a detached or an involved position. For example, if you should select a detached approach, you would gain a degree of objectivity by giving an accurate, well-ordered presentation of both sides of the issue and by declaring your position with formal, controlled logic. If, on the other hand, you should assume an involved position, either pro or con, your presentation should be more persuasive, more demanding. You would need to avoid bias and prejudice, but you could be more subjective by condemning falsehoods, by destroying misconceptions, by rallying your audience to your cause, and by supporting your ideas with examples and comparisons that vividly portray the circumstances.

Moreover, with some topics you should consider the possibility of a humorous or a satiric approach, by which you relate, with tongue in cheek, the absurdity of a situation or you hold up to ridicule the foolishness of a condition, intending, thereby, to bring a new awareness of a problem to your reader.

Finally, ask yourself, "Do I have sufficient support from several sources for my contentions?" Since many undergraduates attempt to rely upon one major source, this question is a vital one. Remember, reliance upon the frequent use of one source is an all-too apparent confession that your research has been too restricted in its scope. The presence of almost endless strings of "Ibid." entries in your footnotes reflects a lack of industry and initiative on your part. The footnotes of your text, as well as the text itself, will reflect the quality of your research. Your instructor expects that you will put labor into collecting and assimilating adequate material from many sources and that you will then blend these sources into a readable and effective whole.

Writing Your Paper

After many hours of considerable effort, you are ready to give expression to your ideas, to share them with others, and to convince your reader of the validity of your findings. In order for your paper to reflect the care and time you have devoted to it, you must write it in the best possible language. In most instances, the reader will see only the finished product, upon which he will base his judgment of your findings and writing ability. Therefore, you should carefully construct your paragraphs, seek variety and emphasis in your sentences, and select words properly.

PARAGRAPH UNITY

You should develop only one main idea in each of your paragraphs. This rule may seem obvious; yet many students fail to follow it, expecting instead that their own mind will control the order of their presentation. Sometimes this method is successful, but most writers need exterior guidelines. The most useful guide and control of paragraph development is the topic sentence.

Appearing most often as the first sentence of your paragraph, the topic sentence points the direction of your main idea and indicates paragraph content. For example, note this sample topic sentence from the "Billy Budd" paper (pp. 80–96):

```
One of Melville's first biblical comparisons is that of
Billy Budd to Adam.
```

The key words of this sentence are "One . . . [comparison] . . . is . . . Billy Budd to Adam." The paragraph must develop the idea of the comparison; it may not develop an idea of other characters in the novel, such as Captain Vere or Claggart, or other biblical characters, such as Abraham or Joseph. The full paragraph, as it appears in the paper, follows:

```
        One of Melville's first biblical com-

parisons is that of Billy Budd to Adam.  Mel-

ville portrays Billy as "a sort of upright

barbärian, much such perhaps as Adam pre-

sumably might have been ere the urbane Serpent

wriggled himself into his company."4

Melville also describes him as possessing an

amiable disposition, never giving offense to

anyone.5 And, the author says that Billy

"had none of that intuitive knowledge of

the bad. . . ."6
```

By citing Melville himself, the student has developed the idea of the one comparison.

Next, compare a set of topic sentences:

A. Billy, like Adam, falls from grace.

B. Melville develops the fact that Billy's fall, like
   Adam's, was inevitable and unavoidable.

Which is a better topic sentence? Sentence A presents the idea of Billy's fall, but it is too general because it offers no direction or restriction. In contrast, Sentence B is a good topic sentence because it narrows the idea of the paragraph to the inevitability of the fall.

Look next at these topic sentences:

A. Melville develops a comparison of Billy and Claggart
   with David and Saul.

B. Melville develops a comparison of Billy and Claggart
   with David and Saul to reinforce a point: the
   envy of Claggart is a deeper, more pervading evil
   than Saul's.

There should be no doubt in your mind that Sentence B is better because it restricts the paragraph to the main idea of Claggart's envy as revealed by the comparison. A student using Sentence A as his topic sentence might eventually get to the point, but he also runs the danger of missing it entirely.

PARAGRAPH EXPANSION

Writing a good topic sentence is one thing, expanding its main idea is another. For example, suppose we have the following topic sentence:

```
Melville's allegorical treatment of Billy reveals that
man does not remain completely innocent and therefore
will fall from grace.
```

In developing the full paragraph, you could expand upon the idea of the "allegorical treatment," the "loss of innocence," or "the fall of man." In addition, you could choose any one of several rhetorical methods of paragraph development, as shown below. In other words, you may wish to write, in your notes, several rhetorical alternatives for a purpose statement, such as:

```
I will develop this topic sentence by presenting:

    a. examples of the allegorical treatment.
    b. the meaning of the term "allegorical treatment."
    c. the causes for the fall of man.
    d. the results of the fall of man.
    e. both the cause and effect of man's fall.
    f. a comparison of Billy and all other men.
```

Obviously, you have multiple opportunities for expansion of the topic sentence. Your use of illustrations will provide specific, concrete details of an abstract idea. Definition enables you to make your reader aware of what *you* mean by a term such as "allegorical treatment" or "loss of innocence." Or, if you place emphasis on a cause or an effect, you will examine the *why* of an idea. Your use of comparison enables you to distinguish between the similarities and the differences of two ideas, events, or objects.

In addition, you may add strength and structure to your argument by calling upon recognized authorities, that is, by citing the primary source (Melville) or secondary sources (those who write about Melville). Furthermore, this supporting data may also consist of statistics, tables, and graphs (see pp. 142–46) in research papers that treat such topics as "the population explosion," "germination of bacterial spores," "big city ghettoes," or "mental illness of teen-agers." Other possibilities for expansion are explication and analysis, in which case you would examine and explain, say, Melville's allegorical treatment of Billy Budd.

PARAGRAPH COHERENCE

Your attention to paragraph unity and expansion will determine, to a great extent, the coherence of your paragraph. You should so order your material that the reader will have no difficulty in following and understanding the logical progression of your ideas, from the controlling idea of your topic sentence to the complete expansion of secondary ideas. Note again this sample paragraph:

One of Melville's first biblical comparisons is that of Billy Budd to Adam. Melville portrays Billy as "a sort of upright barbarian, much such perhaps as Adam presumably might have been ere the urbane Serpent wriggled himself into his company."[4] Melville also describes him as possessing an amiable disposition, never giving offense to anyone.[5] And, the author says that Billy "had none of that intuitive knowledge of the bad. . . ."[6]

The writer achieves paragraph coherence by his maintenance of one controlling idea, Billy's comparison to Adam, and by his expansion, the citations from Melville. He gains additional coherence by repeating key words, using pronouns and synonyms, forming parallel sentence structures, and inserting transitional words and phrases (for example, *also, furthermore, nevertheless, thus,* and so on). You should use these same devices in your writing.

WRITING EFFECTIVE SENTENCES

You will achieve paragraph unity and coherence only by building effective sentences. As you write your paper, you should carefully consider your sentence syntax; that is, the relationship of words, the need for parallel structure, and the precise use of modifying phrases and clauses, as these syntactic units contribute to effective use of loose and periodic sentence patterns.

Normally, you will write the loose sentence, presenting the main clause first and gathering additions to it. Although its rambling structure prevents the emphasis gained by periodic sentences (well-proportioned sentences of several clauses), the loose sentence is natural and efficient. However, if you wish to gain sentence variety and emphasis, you should occasionally alter your normal word order or open up the sentence with modifiers, thereby delaying your main idea until the end of the sentence. That is, a periodic sentence is one in which the central meaning is delayed until the end or near the end of the sentence. As a result, your periodic sentences will suspend the reader's attention across the accumulated material. And, since the reader will subconsciously anticipate the main idea to come, you thereby bring the main idea into sharp focus. The following sentences demonstrate a few methods of building both the loose and the periodic sentence:

Participial phrase

Loose: Captain Vere becomes fond of Billy Budd, loving him as a son.

Periodic: Recognizing the essential innocence of the handsome young sailor, Captain Vere becomes fond of Billy Budd.

Adverb clause

Loose: Captain Vere becomes fond of Billy Budd when he recognizes Billy's innocent nature.

Periodic: When he recognizes Billy's innocent nature, Captain Vere becomes extremely fond of him.

Adverb

Loose: Captain Vere becomes fond of Billy Budd early in the voyage.

Periodic: Early in the voyage, Captain Vere becomes fond of Billy Budd.

Prepositional phrase

Loose: Captain Vere recognizes the young sailor's basic innocence on the day of Billy's arrival aboard the ship.

Periodic: On the first day of Billy's stay aboard the vessel, Captain Vere recognizes the young sailor's basic innocence.

Noun cluster

Loose: Captain Vere becomes fond of Billy Budd, a young, innocent sailor.

Periodic: A gentle, kind man at heart, Captain Vere becomes fond of Billy Budd.

Multiple phrases and clauses

Loose: Billy strikes Claggart a mortal blow because he needs an outlet for his terrible wrath after hearing Claggart accuse him of mutiny.

Periodic: Because he needs an outlet for his terrible wrath after hearing Claggart accuse him of mutiny, Billy strikes Claggart a mortal blow.

SUBORDINATE SENTENCE ELEMENTS

The sentences above provide examples of the multiple uses of modifying phrases and clauses. Since you need these subordinate ideas in your sentences and since they cannot stand alone, you must place them carefully so that they modify the correct word or idea. Note the following:

```
When Claggart accuses him of mutiny, Billy, suddenly
speechless, strikes Claggart with his fist.
```

The main idea, "Billy strikes Claggart," serves as the main clause, while the subordinate units, logically positioned, modify an idea in the main clause. "Suddenly speechless" modifies the subject "Billy" and "When Claggart accuses him of mutiny" modifies the verb "strikes." But notice what may happen if you forget to subordinate your minor ideas:

```
Claggart accuses Billy of mutiny, and Billy suddenly
becomes speechless. He strikes Claggart with his fist.
```

Grammatically we cannot argue with these sentences, but rhetorically we realize that the writer has given equal expression and structure to all ideas, even the minor ones. Thus, you should realize that precise handling of sentence elements requires two considerations: a recognition of your major and minor ideas and the proper placing of them within the sentence structure.

USING ACTIVE VOICE

Preferably, you should write in the active voice rather than in the passive. Note the following:

```
A. Billy Budd is called an innocent sailor by Melville.
```

```
B. Melville calls Billy Budd an innocent sailor.
```

Notice that the subject of Sentence A, "Billy Budd," receives the action, while in Sentence B the subject, "Melville," acts. Active voice is strong and dynamic; passive voice is weak because the actor is lost in a prepositional phrase or omitted altogether.

FORMING PARALLEL STRUCTURES

By recognizing ideas of equal importance and by giving them identical grammatical constructions, you can achieve a harmonious balance of words, phrases, and clauses. The creation of parallel structure will mark you as a proficient writer. Note the following:

```
Billy enters the cabin and joins Claggart in front of
Captain Vere's desk. Claggart then accuses Billy of
mutiny.
```

By joining two words into a compound structure, the writer can gain sentence balance and word economy:

```
Both Billy and Claggart stand before Captain Vere as
Claggart accuses Billy of mutiny.
```

In the next pair of sentences the writer gains balance in Sentence B by forming two equal phrases:

```
A. Listening first to Claggart's accusation, Captain
     Vere then watches Billy's violent reaction, and
     Vere thus becomes a partner in a drama that he
     cannot solve and cannot ignore.

B. Listening first to Claggart's accusation and
     witnessing next Billy's violent reaction, Captain
     Vere unwillingly becomes a partner in a tragic
     drama that he can neither escape nor resolve.
```

You may also gain parallelism by forming two equal clauses:

```
A. Claggart accuses Billy of mutiny after trying to
     entice him into evil because he cannot accept
     Billy's inherent goodness.

B. When he cannot entice Billy into evil and when he can
     no longer accept Billy's inherent goodness, Claggart
     accuses Billy of mutiny.
```

The balanced, periodic structure of Sentence B provides clarity and precision.

USING WORDS EFFECTIVELY

By carefully selecting the specific word, you will create for your reader an exact image, a clarity often absent if you use vague, general words. For example, words such as *kill, murder,* and *slay* express in abstract terms such concrete acts as *strangle, poison, drown, stab,* and *shoot to death.* Note the following:

```
Billy Budd kills Claggart.
```

The reader, left to his own imagination, can form his own idea of the deed. But note the following version:

```
With his fist, Billy Budd strikes Claggart a mortal blow.
```

The writer of this sentence clarifies and makes specific Billy's action. Thus, as a general rule, you should seek the specific, concrete word and avoid the vague, general one.

Also, you should avoid overworked words. Note the following sentences:

```
Catch [grab, snare] the ball.

Catch [overtake] that other car.

Catch [hook, net, land] a fish.

Catch [detect] him in the act.

Catch [arrest, apprehend] the robber.
```

Clearly, the word *catch* is overworked. There are nine other words that could easily replace *catch* in these sentences. By referring often to a good dictionary (see p. 6), you may add variety to your word choice.

In addition, you must consider the nuances of the language. You have at your command a large supply of words, any of which might be used, but usually one word is better than another. For example, consider the word choices in the following:

$$\text{Standing} \begin{Bmatrix} \text{disdainfully} \\ \text{deceitfully} \\ \text{defiantly} \end{Bmatrix} \text{before Captain Vere, the} \begin{Bmatrix} \text{evil} \\ \text{satanic} \\ \text{crazed} \end{Bmatrix}$$

$$\text{Claggart} \begin{Bmatrix} \text{accuses} \\ \text{indicts} \\ \text{charges} \end{Bmatrix} \text{Billy Budd of} \begin{Bmatrix} \text{insurrection} \\ \text{mutiny} \\ \text{revolt} \end{Bmatrix}$$

The words in each group of synonyms have almost the same denotative value because their referents are the same or similar, but the words of each group differ slightly in connotation. Your purpose and audience should dictate your word choice.

Conversely, you will use other words that look or sound alike but that actually have distinct meanings. When doubtful about the correct usage of any of the following words, you should consult a dictionary:

accept, except	forth, fourth
adapt, adopt	imply, infer
adverse, averse	in, into
advice, advise	instance, instants
affect, effect	its, it's
allude, elude	judicial, judicious
allusion, illusion	later, latter
already, all ready	loose, lose
altogether, all together	moral, morale
almost, most	passed, past
born, borne, bourn	precede, proceed
capital, capitol	principal, principle
censor, censure	quiet, quite
cite, site, sight	respectably, respectfully,
coarse, course	respectively
complement, compliment	shone, shown
continual, continuous	statue, statute, stature
credible, credulous	than, then
desert, dessert	their, they're, there
economic, economical	threw, through
fewer, less	to, too, two
formally, formerly	who's, whose

In searching for colorful, expressive words, you may employ the simile or metaphor. Both suggest a comparison between two unlike things. The metaphor implies an analogy; for example, "Claggart is satanic" or "Claggart is a serpent." The simile expresses the comparison with the words *like, as,* or *than;* for example, "Claggart is like Satan" or

"Claggart is sly as a serpent." At the same time, however, you should avoid clichés and trite expressions, as in the following:

```
At the crack of dawn, Billy Budd stood trembling in a
cold sweat when, like a bolt from the blue, death
reared its ugly head; and Billy, not the least of those
who have gone to a watery grave, passed away into the
great beyond.
```

No less than seven clichés appear in the above sentence.

Furthermore, you should avoid pretentious, flowery language. Euphemisms, for example, may be useful to replace distasteful words, as when *passed away* is used in place of *died*. But euphemisms may also distort an idea or image, as when *bill collectors* are *adjusters, undertakers* are *morticians, jobs* are *positions, old folks* are *senior citizens,* the *poor* are *underprivileged* or *culturally deprived, sweat* is *perspiration, garbage* is *refuse,* the *city dump* is a *sanitary land fill,* a *depression* is a *recession,* and *janitors* are *sanitary engineers* or *building superintendents.* In short, you should strive for the exact, definitive word, realizing, however, that appropriateness may often require the more pleasant word, for example, *odor* rather than *stink.*

EMPHASIS

If you write with clarity, you should seldom need intensification. Note the following:

```
Billy himself faces the bitterest of struggles; signifi-
cantly, however, he approaches his very death with
tremendous courage.
```

Since an intelligent reader will react unfavorably to such extremism, you should guard against an abundance of intensifiers, such as *measurably, significantly, considerably, colossal, stupendous, tremendous, super,* and *very.* Simple, direct phrasing is usually more effective and meaningful, for example:

```
With an unusual serenity, Billy faces his death.
```

At the same time, you should guard against an overuse of external devices of emphasis, such as underlining, double underlining, wavy underlining, and exclamation marks.

Finally, the repetition of words is effective if used properly, as in the following:

```
Because he cannot speak, because he cannot control his
anger, because he must defend himself, Billy strikes
Claggart a mortal blow.
```

But unfortunate repetition may result in such writing as:

> Because of a <u>speech</u> impediment, Billy cannot <u>speak</u>;
> therefore, he uses his fist against Claggart instead of
> <u>speaking</u> in his own defense.

In the same way, you should guard against redundancy; that is, do not repeat yourself needlessly, as in:

> Billy is an innocent sailor who is guiltless and
> blameless.

USING THE PROPER TENSE

Since you are dealing with an event or work of the past, your overall approach to the material should be in the past tense:

> John Calvin <u>was</u> <u>born</u> at Noyon, Picardy, on July 10,
> 1509. At the age of fourteen he <u>entered</u> the University
> of Paris and <u>began</u> the study of theology. He <u>completed</u>
> his theological training at nineteen, and then as the
> result of his father's wish, he <u>went</u> to Orleans to
> study law.

Clearly, the use of the past tense is required with this material. But note the opening of the "Billy Budd" paper:

> The Bible has stood for centuries as a
> clarification of what <u>is</u> good and what <u>is</u>
> evil. People at the center of this book
> <u>portray</u> success and failure, righteousness and
> wickedness. In a striking parallel <u>Billy</u> <u>Budd</u>
> <u>possesses</u> many characteristics of the Bible.

The writer of these lines is concerned with two works of the past, but since both books continue in print, they continue into the present. Therefore, the writer uses the verbs *is, portray,* and *possesses* rather than *was, portrayed,* and *possessed.* That is, he uses the historical present tense to indicate what is true at the present time and will remain true in the future.

In the same way, you should use the present tense for most comments or observations upon events in a work under examination. Thus, in a paper on Hawthorne's *The Scarlet Letter,* instead of writing "Dimmesdale *was* weak and indecisive as he *stood* on the platform with Hester and Pearl," you would employ the present tense: "Dimmesdale *is* weak and indecisive as he *stands* on the platform. . . ." Similarly, use the present tense in referring to a view expressed by some quoted or paraphrased author, for the criticism is still in print and continues to be true in the present. Good usage demands "Professor Thompson argues," "Professor Thompson writes," or "Professor Thompson observes," rather than "Professor Thompson argued," "Professor Thompson wrote," or "Professor Thompson observed."

REVISING YOUR FIRST DRAFT

After completing the first draft, begin the revision and rewriting in a critical and exacting mood—there is no place for any complacent pride of accomplishment at this point. Conscientiously delete unnecessary material, add supporting statements and evidence, relate facts to one another, rearrange data, and rewrite. Follow this cycle until the paper meets your full approval. Check for errors in sentence structure, spelling, and punctuation, and read each quotation for accuracy. Finally, check each footnote and bibliography entry for correctness of content and form.

Handling Reference Material

As you begin transferring your note material into your written text, you may have questions about the proper use of your references. For example, you will often ask yourself, "How should I use this note—as paraphrase or quotation?" Obviously, you cannot just copy all your notes directly into the text. The trick is to skillfully incorporate a paraphrase or short quotation into your own writing so that the outside source is not obtrusive and at the same time illuminates and supports your own conclusions. You will find that this task is vital to the success of your manuscript.

SHORT PROSE QUOTATIONS AND PARAPHRASES

There are two basic forms for incorporating quoted matter into the text. First, if the quotation is no more than four lines long, you may place it within the body of the text and enclose it within quotation marks.

Suppose, for example, that you have the following material on a note card:

```
Urban growth in backward countries

R. C. Anderson, SE, 29, 335




"Currently, a rapid rate of urban growth is
one of the most obvious characteristics of the
underdeveloped nation."
```

There are several ways you could incorporate this material into your paper, but not all of them would be considered acceptable. Consider the following example:

Unacceptable

```
        "Currently, a rapid rate of urban growth

   is one of the most obvious characteristics of

   the underdeveloped nation."1  The farmers and

   laborers in Asia, Africa, and Latin America

   are tired of their misery.  They are moving

   to the city, hoping that things will somehow

   be better.


        1Randall C. Anderson, "The Role of Human
   Geography in the Study of Emerging Nations,"
   Social Education, 29 (Oct. 1965), 335.
```

This style would be unacceptable to most teachers because the writer provides no introduction for the quotation.

Acceptable

> The farmers and laborers in Asia, Africa, and Latin America are tired of their misery. They are moving to the city, hoping that things will somehow be better. As Randall C. Anderson notes, "A rapid rate of urban growth is one of the most obvious characteristics of the underdeveloped nation."[1]
>
> [1]"The Role of Human Geography in the Study of Emerging Nations," <u>Social</u> <u>Education</u>, 29 (Oct. 1965), 335.

In this example the writer has adequately introduced the quotation. Other alternatives to this version might be:

. . . will somehow be better; the result, says Randall C. Anderson, is that "a rapid rate of urban growth is. . . ."

. . . will somehow be better. This has led at least one observer to conclude that "a rapid rate of urban growth is. . . ."

Randall C. Anderson points out that "a rapid rate of urban growth is one of the most obvious characteristics of the underdeveloped nation." In other words, farmers and laborers in Asia, Africa, and Latin America are moving. . . .

In the same way, your paraphrases should be properly introduced:

Acceptable

> Tired of their misery, farmers and laborers in Asia, Africa, and Latin America are moving to the city with hopes that things will somehow be better. The result, according to Randall C. Anderson, is a rapid urban growth of these underdeveloped nations.[1]
>
> [1]"The Role of Human Geography in the Study of Emerging Nations," <u>Social</u> <u>Education</u>, 29 (Oct. 1965), 335.

INTRODUCING SHORT QUOTATIONS AND PARAPHRASES

When introducing short reference material (four lines or less), you should avoid repetition of a stereotyped phrase—for example, "Professor Jones says." Rather, you should try to vary the method of formal introduction, as shown in the following:

> According to Newton Arvin, Melville centers his story around. . . .
>
> Raymond Weaver sees <u>Billy</u> <u>Budd</u> as a gospel story filled with crime, sin, punishment. . . .
>
> E. L. Grant Watson insists that Melville uses his characters to hint at. . . .
>
> Melville portrays Billy as "a sort of upright barbarian. . . ."
>
> One critic argues that "there is a mysterious justice in. . . ."
>
> Explaining Billy's tragedy, R. W. B. Lewis declares: "Fortunately, as it turned out, there had been. . . ."
>
> It was "the spirit of truth to see what needed to be done, and the spirit of faithfulness to go and do it," contends one biblical scholar.
>
> Nathalia Wright suggests that the parallel in this allusion can be. . . .
>
> Wright points out that both Billy and Vere "are subject to. . . ."
>
> The price of this social expediency, implies one authority, is a blighting, human mediocrity.

Other words that will give variety to your introductions are *accept, add, admit, affirm, believe, confirm, mention, propose, rely, report, reveal, state, submit, suggest, think,* and *verify.* However, you should avoid the monotony of such introductions by alternating them with your own contentions and with a few long single-spaced quotations (see below, "Longer Quotations," p. 70).

COMBINING PARAPHRASE AND QUOTATION

As shown above, it is a good practice to introduce your material by citing the name of the authority from which it is drawn. However, you must place a footnote index numeral at the end of paraphrased and quoted matter whether the name of the author appears in the text or not. In the following example the writer of the "Billy Budd" paper has obeyed these two rules. Additionally, he has molded into one unified paragraph both paraphrase and quotation:

Wendell Glick provides the most logical
answer to the moral dilemma by stressing that
Melville deplores with Vere the injustice that
finds Billy condemned.[28] Glick argues that
justice to the individual, according to
Melville's story, is not "the ultimate loyalty
in a complex culture."[29] He states that "the
stability of the culture has a higher claim,
and when the two conflict, justice to the
individual must be abrogated to keep the order
of society intact."[30]

[28]"Expediency and Absolute Morality in
Billy Budd," PMLA, 68 (March 1953), 104.

[29]Ibid.

[30]Ibid.

You cannot paraphrase and synthesize such material into the desired
context without intelligent, thoughtful effort. To provide an indication
of the care that is required, the writer's note card is supplied below:

Captain Vere   Glick, 104

    "Melville sympathized with Billy Budd
as completely as did Captain Vere. He appre-
ciated with the Captain the stark injustice
of a situation which finds the individual
condemned for adherence to a standard of
behavior most men would consider noble and
right. But he agreed with the Captain that
justice to the individual is not the ultimate
loyalty in a complex culture; the stability
of the culture has a higher claim, and when
the two conflict, justice to the individual
must be abrogated to keep the order of society
intact . . . . Melville and Captain Vere
brought in the verdict that the claims of
civilized society may upon occasion constitute
a higher ethic than the claims of 'natural
law' and personal justice."

REPRODUCING QUOTED MATERIAL

In general, you should reproduce quoted material exactly; but one exception is permitted for logical reasons: if the quotation forms a grammatical part of the sentence in which it occurs, you need not capitalize the first word of the quotation, even though it is capitalized in the original, as in:

```
Frederic I. Carpenter agrees that "the traditional
answer remains clear, but the romantic and the
idealistic have usually been confused."17
```

However, if the quotation follows a formal introduction, you should capitalize the first word as in the original:

```
Frederic I. Carpenter identifies an area of confusion
when he declares: "The traditional answer remains clear,
but the romantic and the idealistic have usually been
confused."17
```

Thus, a few rules for quoted material of four lines or less are:

1. Reproduce the quotation exactly as it appears in the original with the one exception noted above.

2. Place the material within quotation marks.

3. Insert a footnote numeral after the last word of the material.

4. Use the name of the authority, usually, to introduce the material. Items 3 and 4 apply with equal force to your paraphrases.

If your paper is based solely on a single novel or short story and if there is one footnote identifying the edition, you may employ a simpler method of documentation for citations of the primary source; that is, place the page numbers in parentheses after the prose quotations, for example:

```
    Melville portrays Billy as "a sort of upright

    barbarian, much such perhaps as Adam presuma-

    bly might have been ere the urbane Serpent

    wriggled himself into his company" (p. 52).1

    Melville also describes him as possessing an

    amiable disposition, never giving offense to

    anyone (p. 68).


        1Citations from Melville in the text
    are to Billy Budd, Sailor (An Inside Narra-
    tive), ed. Harrison Hayford and Merton M.
    Sealts, Jr. (Chicago: Univ. of Chicago Press,
    1962).
```

LONGER QUOTATIONS

Quotations that exceed four lines should be indented and single-spaced.[1] But do not overuse long quotations. The obvious fact is that most readers tend to skip over long single-spaced material unless it is strongly introduced and unless such quotations occur infrequently. The proper method for such quotations is shown below:

```
         Melville develops a comparison of Billy

    and Claggart with David and Saul to reinforce

    a point: the envy of Claggart is a deeper,

    more pervading evil than Saul's.  Melville

    states:

              But Claggart's was no vulgar form of the
         passion.  Nor, as directed toward Billy
         Budd, did it partake of that streak of
         apprehensive jealousy that marred Saul's
         visage perturbedly brooding on the comely
         young David.  Claggart's envy struck
         deeper.11

    So Melville wished to go farther than merely

    the parallel of jealousy in Saul and Claggart

    against. . . .
```

As indicated in this example, you should observe the following rules:

1. Do not employ quotation marks with a long quotation that is single-spaced and indented.

2. Place the footnote index numeral, as always, after the last word of the quotation.

3. Indent the material at least five spaces from the left margin and provide at least one line space both above and below the material.

4. If quoted matter begins with the opening of a paragraph, indent the first line at least ten spaces from the left margin; the quotation, that is, carries its own paragraph indentation. Otherwise there is no extra indentation of the first line.

5. Finally, make certain that the quotation is properly introduced. Use a colon to link the quotation with its introduction.

POETRY QUOTATIONS

Short passages of quoted poetry are included in the text in the following manner:

---

[1] In this instance, your instructor may request that you follow strictly the stipulations of the *MLA Style Sheet* for articles to be published: that is, set off only quotations of 100 words or more and double space all quotations.

```
    In Antony and Cleopatra Shakespeare states his

    theme at once through the indignant, hard-

    natured Roman soldier Philo, who labels Antony

    "the triple pillar of the world transformed /

    Into a strumpet's fool" (Antony I.i.12-13).

    Philo thereby heralds the traditional moral

    attitude of the Roman mind as opposed by the

    sensuous nature of Egypt and its queen.
```

As this example indicates, you should again follow certain rules:

1. Set off the quotation by quotation marks.

2. Indicate two separate lines of the poetry text by the use of a virgule (/).

3. Place the documentation in parentheses immediately following the quotation.

4. Insert the documentation inside the period because the reference, like the quotation, is a part of the larger context of the sentence.

5. Omit the footnote. But be certain that the quotation is properly introduced.

6. Good scholarship requires that the edition of Shakespeare's plays, or any similar anthology, be listed in an early footnote entry, for example:

```
    1Citations from Shakespeare in the text are to
Shakespeare:  Twenty-Three Plays and the Sonnets, ed.
Thomas M. Parrott (New York:  Scribner's, 1953).
```

Longer passages of poetry are handled differently, as shown by the following passage from Shakespeare's *Hamlet*.

```
    In a famous soliloquy Hamlet declares:

    To be, or not to be: that is the question:
    Whether 't is nobler in the mind to suffer
    The slings and arrows of outrageous fortune,
    Or to take arms against a sea of troubles,
    And by opposing end them?  To die, to sleep--
    No more; and by a sleep to say we end
    The heart-ache and the thousand natural shocks
    That flesh is heir to. . . . (Ham. III.i.56-63)
```

Also notice the form of documentation for the following:

```
    In his poem "Among School Children," W. B. Yeats

    asks two profound questions:

        Are you the leaf, the blossom or the
            bole?
        O body swayed to music, O brightening
            glance,
        How can we know the dancer
            from the dance? (11. 62-64)
```

Again, you should follow certain rules:

1. Center the quotation on the page and type with single-spacing and with quotation marks omitted.

2. Use this method whenever poetry quotations run longer than two lines.

3. Place the documentation outside the final period because the reference is not a contextual part of the quoted sentence of poetry.

4. Use a colon to link the quotation with its introduction.

5. Omit the footnote. But, again, good scholarship requires an early footnote that lists the edition or anthology in which the poem is found (see 6 above).

ELLIPSIS

In a situation where less than an entire sentence of the quoted material is needed, you should use ellipsis dots to indicate omissions in the quoted material. This mark is three spaced periods, as (. . .). When the ellipsis ends a quoted passage, you should add a fourth period (with no space before the first) to indicate the termination of thought. Note the following:

```
    R. W. B. Lewis declares that "if Hester has sinned, she
    has done so as an affirmation of life, and her sin is
    the source of life. . . ."1

    One critic insists that it is possible "to read The
    Scarlet Letter . . . as an indorsement of hopeful-
    ness. . . ."1

    Phil Withim objects to the idea that "such episodes are
    intended to demonstrate that Vere . . . has the intelli-
    gence and insight to perceive the deeper issue.'1
```

If the omission is significant (one or more lines of verse or one or more paragraphs of prose), indicate the ellipsis by a single typed line of spaced periods.

BRACKETS

You may find it necessary, on occasion, to insert personal comment within a quotation. You should enclose such an interpolation within brackets. Note the following:

```
"The black flower [of society] is shown in striking
contrast to the wild rose of Nature."

One critic indicates that "we must avoid the temptation
to read it [The Scarlet Letter] heretically."

"John F. Kennedy, assassinated in November of 1964 [sic],
became overnight an immortal figure of courage and dig-
nity in the hearts of all Americans."

"John F. Kennedy, . . . [was] an immortal figure of
courage and dignity in the hearts of all Americans."
```

Format

In its basic organization the research paper consists of the following parts:
1. One blank page
2. Title page
3. Outline (if required)
4. Body
5. Bibliography
6. One blank page

THE TITLE PAGE

The title page contains three main divisions: the title of the work, the author, and the class information. Note the following guidelines for title pages:

1. If the title requires two or more lines, position the extra line(s) in such a manner as to form an inverted pyramid.

2. Capitalize, do not underline, the title. Also, do not use a period after a centered heading.

3. Enter your own name with the word "by" directly above it.

4. Provide the class and section information and the date. Entry of the instructor's name is usually optional.

5. Employ separate lines for each item.

6. Provide balanced, two-inch margins for all sides of the title page. Remember, the primary requirement for the title page is that the material be arranged into a well-balanced page. Two examples follow:

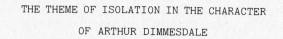

THE THEME OF ISOLATION IN THE CHARACTER

OF ARTHUR DIMMESDALE

**Fig. 37: Sample
Title Page**

by

James B. Johnson

Freshman English II, Section 108C

Mr. Stewart

April 24, 1970

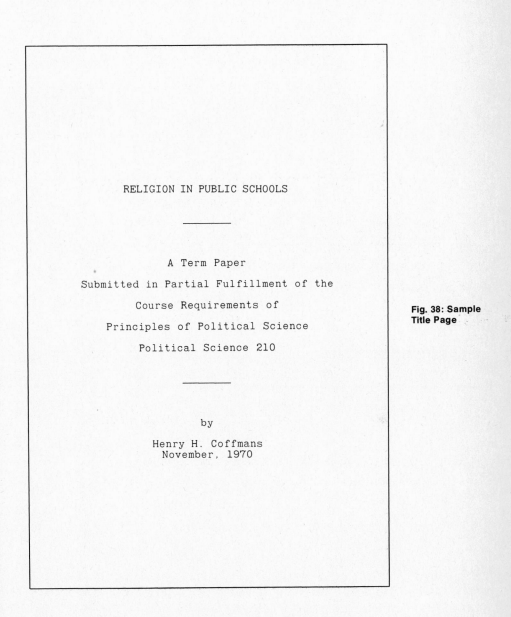

RELIGION IN PUBLIC SCHOOLS

————

A Term Paper
Submitted in Partial Fulfillment of the
Course Requirements of
Principles of Political Science
Political Science 210

————

by
Henry H. Coffmans
November, 1970

Fig. 38: Sample Title Page

(For another sample title page, see p. 81.)

THE OUTLINE

The outline follows the title page in the finished manuscript, its pages being numbered with small Roman numerals (for example, iii, iv, v) in the top, right-hand corner of the page (see also "Outlining," pp. 35–39 and 50–53).

THE BODY OF THE RESEARCH PAPER

The body of the paper is obviously the most important part of your work. You should therefore be certain that your format conforms to the stipulations set forth below. (See also individual items in the "Glossary of Research Terms," pp. 139–48.)

CHAPTERS

Omit divisions altogether or separate them by subtitles or side heads (see "Subtitles" below). Divide the paper into chapters only when you have a long, complex presentation.

CONCLUSION

Normally, the final summarizing paragraph of the text will be sufficient, although special circumstances may, on occasion, demand a separate conclusion. For instance, the writer of the "Billy Budd" research paper presents a formal, five-paragraph conclusion (see pp. 92–95) in order to summarize the several comparisons between the Bible and *Billy Budd.*

FOOTNOTE NUMERALS

Place footnote numerals within the text of the paper by turning the platen of the typewriter so that the numeral strikes about half a space above the line. Each numeral immediately follows the quotation or material to which it refers (see also "Placing Footnote Numbers Within the Text," p. 99).

FOOTNOTES

Footnotes appear on the same page as do the footnote index numerals in your text. Separate the footnotes from the text by triple spacing (that is, leave two lines of space). Single space the footnotes, indent each as a paragraph, and double space between each note. (However, your instructor may ask that you follow strictly the stipulations of the *MLA Style Sheet*: that is, double space your footnotes and place them, not at the bottom of each page, but all together on separate sheets at the end of your paper.)

INTRODUCTION

An introductory section is seldom necessary in the undergraduate paper; the opening paragraph(s) of the text will normally be sufficient.

However, include a separate introduction to explain unusual circumstances about an investigation.

ITALICS

Indicate italics in a typed manuscript by underlining. Always underline the title of a book, journal, or periodical, whether it appears in the text, in a footnote, or in the bibliography. Also underline the titles of pamphlets, newspapers, plays, movies, long poems, and operas. In addition, underline foreign words (except proper names, quotations in a foreign language, titles of articles in a foreign language, and other foreign words anglicized through usage). Conversely, enclose within quotation marks titles of articles, essays, chapters, sections, short poems, stories, and songs. Also underline words or phrases which are out of normal context or which are being emphasized.

LENGTH OF THE RESEARCH PAPER

Generally speaking, plan a paper of 2000 or 3000 words, about ten typewritten pages, excluding the title page, outline, and bibliography. However, your instructor may set definite restrictions concerning the length of the paper. Various factors make it difficult to set an arbitrary length, which may well vary with the topic, the reference material available, the time allotted to the project, and the initiative of the student.

MARGINS

The following margin requirements are recommended:

Left margin:	$1\frac{1}{2}$ inches
Right margin:	1 inch
Bottom margin:	1 inch
Top margin:	$1\frac{1}{2}$ inches

Establish the top margin nine spaces below the top of a typewritten page. Place the page number seven spaces below the top of the page and in line with the right margin. However, the top margin for pages with major headings is two inches (about 14 spaces) from the top of the page.

NUMBERING

Assign a number to each page of the paper, except the blank pages. Number the paper in Arabic numerals in the upper right-hand corner of the page, seven spaces down from the top edge of the page and one inch from the right edge. Number these pages consecutively from the first page of the text through the bibliography. However, do not place a number on your first page—though this page is of course counted. Number the pages before the first page of the text, except the title page, with small Roman numerals, e.g., iii, iv, v, and so on, at the top, right side of the page.

PAPER

Type on one side of white bond paper, 16 or 20 pound weight, $8\frac{1}{2}$ x 11. If your final manuscript is in longhand, use ruled theme paper.

SHORT TITLES IN THE TEXT

Shorten titles mentioned often in the text after a first, full reference. For example, *English as Language: Backgrounds, Developments, Usage* should be shortened, after initial usage, to *English as Language*, both in the text and footnotes (see pp. 113–15).

SPACING

Double space the body of the paper. However, single space both the footnotes and bibliography, with double spacing between each entry. Also, indent and single space long quotations, omitting quotation marks. In addition, triple space between a major heading and your text. (However, your instructor may request that you double space everything—text, indented quotations, footnotes, and bibliography entries.)

SPELLING

Spell accurately. When in doubt, always consult a dictionary. If the dictionary says a word may be spelled in two separate ways, be consistent in the form employed, as with *theatre* and *theater*, unless the variant form occurs in quoted materials. Use American spelling throughout. In addition, proofread carefully for hyphenation errors.

SUBTITLES

Rather than chapter divisions, use subtitles, centered on the page, or side heads, underlined and flush with the left margin. Both require at least one line space both above and below. Neither requires that a new page be started (see, for example, the side heads of the "Billy Budd" research paper, pp. 80–96).

TYPING

Preferably, you should submit the paper in typed form, although most instructors will accept handwritten manuscripts, if neat and legible. Also, use pica type, though the small elite face may be used if necessary. Before starting the final copy, clean the type carefully and insert a new ribbon if necessary.

PROOFREADING

You should proofread carefully after the final copy is finished, remembering that you, and you alone, are responsible for everything within the paper. Failure to proofread is an act of carelessness that may seriously lower your final grade. Typing a paper does not remove the requirement of proofreading; if anything it doubles your responsibility, whether you have done the typing yourself or had it done. Typographical errors are mistakes that will often count against the paper just as heavily as other shortcomings. Should errors be found and time does not permit retyping, you should make the necessary corrections neatly in ink. It is far better to mar a page with a few corrections than to leave damaging errors in the paper.

SAMPLE RESEARCH PAPER

AN INTERPRETATION OF MELVILLE'S

USE OF BIBLICAL CHARACTERS

IN <u>BILLY</u> <u>BUDD</u>

by

Doris Singleton

Freshman English II.   Section 108B

Mr.   Crampton

April 23, 1970

AN INTERPRETATION OF MELVILLE'S

USE OF BIBLICAL CHARACTERS

IN <u>BILLY</u> <u>BUDD</u>

OUTLINE

The title is repeated at the beginning of the outline

Thesis sentence: Melville uses biblical references to support his interpretation of the
moral issues that govern men's lives.

Preferably, the thesis sentence should be placed at the beginning of the outline.

  I. The Bible and <u>Billy</u> <u>Budd</u>
    A. The Bible
      1. Righteousness
      2. Wickedness
    B. <u>Billy</u> Budd
      1. A story of man's fall
      2. A gospel story
    C. Biblical references
      1. Characters, ideas, and symbols
      2. Moral issues
        a. Ambiguities
        b. Rights and duties

 II. Billy Budd and Adam
    A. Melville on Billy Budd
      1. "Upright barbarian"
      2. "No cause of offense to anybody"
      3. No "intuitive knowledge of the bad"
    B. Newton Arvin on Billy Budd
      1. His "disarming good nature"
      2. His helplessness in the presence of
        wrong
    C. Billy's inevitable fall
      1. His defect of knowledge
      2. His stutter

There is no need to index the various references placed in the outline. The student obviously has her note cards arranged to fit the outline.

III. Saul and Claggart
    A. Claggart's envy
      1. Melville on Claggart and Saul
      2. Claggart's jealous deceit
    B. Claggart's passion
      1. Recognition of goodness
      2. Inability to share in it

 IV. Joseph and his brothers
    A. Claggart and Joseph's brothers
      1. The brothers' lie
      2. Claggart's lie
    B. Billy and Joseph
      1. Joseph's trust in God
      2. Billy's trust in Captain Vere

V. Abraham and Isaac
   A. Vere and Abraham
      1. Abraham's obedience to God
      2. Vere's obedience to the law
   B. Loyalty to a sovereign power
      1. Spiritual necessity
      2. Social necessity

VI. Symbolic meaning of _Billy Budd_
   A. Symbolism of major characters
      1. Billy's innocence
      2. Claggart's evil
      3. Vere's conscience
   B. Social expediency
      1. Justice to the individual
      2. Loyalty to society
   C. Individual morality
      1. Submission to corruption
      2. Destruction by evil
   D. Billy's death
      1. Image of crucifixion
      2. Image of man's suffering

The title is repeated
on the first page of
the body.

AN INTERPRETATION OF MELVILLE'S

USE OF BIBLICAL CHARACTERS

IN <u>BILLY</u> <u>BUDD</u>

The Bible has stood for centuries as a clarification of what is good and what is evil. People at the
center of this book portray success and failure, right-
eousness and wickedness. In a striking parallel, <u>Billy</u>
<u>Budd</u> possesses many characteristics of the Bible. Ac-
cording to Newton Arvin, Melville centers his story
around the "fall of man and the loss of Paradise."[1]
Raymond Weaver sees it as a gospel story filled with
crime, sin, punishment, love, and innocence, or of vir-
tue versus vice, in which evil and horror are given
their fullest play.[2]

Throughout his tale, Melville intentionally uses
biblical references as a means of portraying and distin-
guishing various characters, ideas, and symbols, and of
presenting different moral principles by which we should
govern our lives. E. L. Grant Watson insists that Melville uses his characters to hint at a "deep and solemn

In lines 6–8 the
student is careful
to introduce her
quotation and
paraphrase with
the name of the
authorities.

Your instructor
may request that
you double space
your footnotes.

[1]<u>Herman</u> <u>Melville</u>: <u>A</u> <u>Critical</u> <u>Biography</u> (New
York: Viking Press, 1950), p. 294.

[2]"Introduction," <u>The</u> <u>Shorter</u> <u>Novels</u> <u>of</u> <u>Herman</u>
<u>Melville</u> (1928; rpt. New York: Premier-Fawcett,
1960), pp. 37-38.

purpose, one no less ambitious than to portray those ambiguities of good and evil as the mutually dependent opposites, between which the world of realization finds its being."[3] The reader therefore discovers, below the surface, the struggles and passions that good and evil involve.

As a result of the parallelism which exists between the biblical references and his own characters, Melville reveals hidden personality traits and the innermost feelings of men possessed of a moral sense and aware of their social obligations.

Billy Budd as Adam

One of Melville's first biblical comparisons is that of Billy Budd to Adam. Melville portrays Billy as "a sort of upright barbarian, much such perhaps as Adam presumably might have been ere the urbane Serpent wriggled himself into his company."[4] Melville also describes him as possessing an amiable disposition, never giving offense to anyone.[5] And the author also says

[3]"Melville's Testament of Acceptance," New England Quarterly, 6 (June 1933), 319-20.

[4]Herman Melville, Billy Budd, Sailor (An Inside Narrative), ed. Harrison Hayford and Merton M. Sealts, Jr. (Chicago: Univ. of Chicago Press. 1962), p. 52.

[5]Ibid., p. 68.

The student has used side heads effectively to divide the sections of her paper.

The organization of each section is excellent. The student introduces the comparison, explicates the material, and then draws conclusions.

The footnotes run consecutively. They are not numbered anew on each page.

Some professors will require you to underline "Ibid." See p. 113n.

that Billy "had none of that intuitive knowledge of the bad. . . . "[6]

Billy is thereby pictured as an innocent youth without malice or deceitfulness. He has no knowledge of the "seamy" side of life. Arvin sees Billy's goodness as "an active and disarming good nature" that wins the affection of the other sailors.[7] But Arvin stresses that the purity of Billy's innocence adds to his helplessness in the presence of wrong.[8]

Along with this comparison, Melville develops the fact that Billy's fall, like Adam's, was inevitable and unavoidable. Both Adam and Billy are limited in their nature by a defect of knowledge. Melville provides, in Billy's stutter, a distinct symbol of his limitation. Arvin argues that "there is a mysterious justice in the fact that this stutter is his [Billy's] undoing."[9] Explaining Billy's tragedy, R. W. B. Lewis declares:

> Fortunately, as it turned out, there had been a fall. Happily, there had been a sin. And, consequently, there had followed the long story of educative experience. All of that experience was at the disposal of each new

[6]Melville, p. 86.

[7]Herman Melville, p. 294.

[8]Ibid.

[9]Ibid., p. 295.

The student properly uses brackets to clarify the pronoun in the Arvin quotation.

Your instructor may request that you double space indented quotations

4

member of the race. The new member inherited the corruption, but he likewise shared in wisdom. If he could never regain Adam's radical innocence, he need never regress to Adam's ignorance.10

Melville's allegorical treatment of Billy therefore reveals that man does not remain completely innocent and will fall. And as man benefited from the sin of Adam, so likewise, from the death of Billy the sailors learn to accept knowledge and authority, and thereby to become better men.

David and Saul

Melville develops a comparison of Billy and Claggart with David and Saul to reinforce a point: the envy of Claggart is a deeper, more pervading evil than was Saul's. Melville states:

But Claggart's was no vulgar form of the passion. Nor, as directed toward Billy Budd, did it partake of that streak of apprehensive jealousy that marred Saul's visage perturbedly brooding on the comely young David. Claggart's envy struck deeper.11

So Melville wished to go farther than merely the parallel of jealousy in Saul and Claggart against the handsome, innocent youths, David and Billy. Saul and Claggart cover their true feelings of hatred toward David and Billy by pretending they are extremely fond of them,

10The American Adam (Chicago: Univ. of Chicago Press, 1955), p. 73.

11Melville, pp. 77–78.

Long quotations are best avoided by the use of paraphrase, but the quotation by Lewis is well phrased and important to the student's argument.

A study of the section about David and Saul will reveal that the student has uncovered no secondary support for her ideas. However, she uses textual materials from the novel to develop an effective interpretation.

87

by directing acts of kindness toward them, and by prais-
ing them with friendly words, when in reality it is
their aim to dispose of them as quickly as possible.

Melville shows that Claggart is not jealous of
Billy as a threat to his own position aboard the ship;
rather, Claggart is jealous of Billy's innocence, which
Claggart cannot share and therefore must destroy.

Melville says that Billy has within himself a spirit that "in its simplicity never willed malice or experienced the reactionary bite of that serpent."[12] The
insight of this spirit intensified the passion of Claggart because "he saw the charm of it, the courageous
free-and-easy temper of it, and fain would have shared
it, but he despaired of it."[13]

In the analogy of Saul and David, Melville suggests
that the evil of Claggart strikes deeply into moral issues. Claggart apprehends the good in Billy, but he is
powerless to share it. Herein lies the tragedy of men
like Claggart. They cannot enjoy the good; they may
only destroy it.

Jacob and Joseph

To make Jacob believe that Joseph is dead, the
brothers kill a lamb and dip the coat in the lamb's

[12]Melville, p. 78.

[13]Ibid.

blood. Carrying the coat to Jacob, the brothers tell
him they could not find Joseph anywhere. One can imagine himself as the spokesman of the group of brothers
standing before Jacob deliberately lying. One would
probably ask the questions, "Will he believe me?" and
"What will he do?" One would undoubtedly have a mixture
of curiosity and apprehension as he awaits the answer.

Claggart is in this situation as he stands before
Captain Vere after accusing Billy of attempted mutiny.
Claggart is described by Melville as having "a look cur-
ious of the operation of his tactics, a look such as
might have been that of the spokesman of the envious
children of Jacob deceptively imposing upon the troubled
patriarch the blood—dyed coat of young Joseph."[14]

But the mention of Joseph and Jacob provides more
than the emotions of Claggart as he stands before Captain Vere. This allusion conveys the underlying motive
of Claggart's aggression against Billy, jealousy, which
is compared with the jealousy the other children of Jacob had for Joseph because he was the father's favorite.

Billy, like Joseph, is punished and imprisoned because of the purity of his innocence. Yet, despite this
unfair trial, Billy believes that Captain Vere is still

[14]Melville, p. 96.

with him, much as Joseph retained his deep-seated faith
and trust that the Lord was with him. Joseph and Billy
show in their controlled and innocent behavior that
there is a spirit in them not present in ordinary men.
It was "the spirit of truth to see what needed to be
done, and the spirit of faithfulness to go and do it,"
contends one biblical scholar.[15]

Abraham and Isaac

To test his devotion, Abraham is commanded by God
to sacrifice his son Isaac upon the altar of God. Abraham lifts the knife to kill Isaac, but God stops him.
Melville alludes to this incident after Vere has virtu-
ally forced the court into finding Billy guilty. Despite a fatherly love for Billy, Vere strictly follows
the law, thereby condemning Billy to death. But Melville adds this observation:

> Captain Vere in end may have developed the passion
> sometimes latent under an exterior stoical or
> indifferent. He was old enough to have been
> Billy's father. The austere devotee of military
> duty, letting himself melt back into what
> remains primeval in our formalized humanity, may
> in end have caught Billy to his heart, even as
> Abraham may have caught young Isaac on the brink
> of resolutely offering him up in obedience to the
> exacting behest.[16]

Captain Vere and Abraham are devoted: Abraham to God

[15]Cuthbert A. Simpson, "Genesis," The Interpreter's
Bible (Nashville: Abingdon Press, 1939), I, 780.

[16]Melville, p. 115.

and Vere to his military obligations. Each is willing
to sacrifice the life of someone he loves.

Nathalia Wright suggests that the parallel in this
allusion can be carried no further.[17] She observes that
"the obedience of Isaac and of Billy Budd are two different things. Isaac was not taken into Abraham's confidence any more than Abraham was taken into Jehovah's.
All is blind obedience, dependent on a jealous and ca-
pricious deity."[18] Vere is obeying the law while main-
taining sympathy for Billy Budd. There is an understanding between the two men. Billy looks to Vere for
guidance and direction, and at his death cries out, "God
bless Captain Vere!"[19] Wright points out that both
Billy and Vere "are subject to a power beyond themselves."[20] Melville never indicates what this power is.
Wright contends it is not simply evil:

> It is beyond good or evil; it is beyond con-
> flict. The realm in which Budd meets Vere is
> not the same as that in which he meets Clag-
> gart, and beyond them all is an utterly
> amoral, mysteriously influential terra incog-
> nita.[21]

This paragraph is an excellent example of paraphrase and quotation of an authority.

[17]Melville's Use of the Bible (Durham: Duke Univ.
Press, 1949), p. 132.

[18]Ibid.

[19]Melville, p. 123.

[20]Melville's Use of the Bible, p. 134.

[21]Ibid.

9

Perhaps if this complex and chaotic world is to remain in a state of peace and order, there must intervene in our lives a sovereign loyalty which must overrule the ordinary reservations of love and affection. The loyalties to God and country deserve "all that a man can give, and in that giving he is blessed," says Cuthbert Simpson.[22] A spiritual and social necessity in obedience is also stressed by Simpson:

> Consider what men have done and will do for their clan or their country. They give their sons to die in battle, to "make the supreme sacrifice." Though they themselves are bereaved, they trust that their nation may be blessed, because through the dedication of young lives the nation may hear the promise which was spoken to Abraham, thy seed shall possess the gate of his enemies.[23]

The fact that God spared Isaac and not Billy shows that the ways of God are sometimes hidden; but ultimately, says Simpson, "his will is found to be not contradictory to the purest emotions planted in human souls."[24]

Conclusion

Each main character in Melville's Billy Budd is compared in at least one way to a biblical character. The biblical characters, by representing good and evil,

Footnote 22 uses no "p." for page because the original footnote, 15, lists a volume number, thereby eliminating usage of "p." (see p. 103).

[22]Simpson, "Genesis," 646.

[23]Ibid.

[24]Ibid.

carry allegorical meanings. Melville uses his comparisons to suggest something hidden, something to be discovered. There are other biblical allusions in the
novel, e.g., to Jonah, Pontius Pilate, and Ananias, but
perhaps the four examined in this paper will suffice to
reveal one interpretation of Melville's meaning.

Billy Budd, as a figure of Adam, David, and Isaac,
represents an innocent person unfamiliar with evil; he
actually thinks Claggart likes him. Claggart is shown
to be representative of Satan. This view is substanti-
ated by the images of Claggart as Saul or as Joseph's
brothers. William Braswell contends that Billy represents the heart and Claggart the head.[25] He argues that
Captain Vere symbolizes the will:

> . . . he is the final authority on all matters
> aboard ship and he determines the ship's
> course of action; he has the ultimate respon-
> sibility of choosing between right and
> wrong.[26]

Braswell's comment suggests that the spiritual issue is
somehow bound by social considerations. Vere understands the injustice of the law, but Braswell states

[25]"Melville's _Billy_ _Budd_ as 'An Inside Narrative,'"
American _Literature_, 29 (May 1957), 134–35.

[26]Braswell, additional note [1960] to "Melville's
Billy _Budd_ as 'An Inside Narrative,'" as quoted in
William T. Stafford, _Melville's_ _Billy_ _Budd_ _and_ _the_
Critics, 2nd ed. (Belmont, Calif.: Wadsworth, 1968),
p. 155.

Note footnote 26.
Stafford's book has
a footnote by Bras-
well that was not in-
cluded in the original
article. (See also
footnote 27 on the
following page.)

that "he sets imperfect order above anarchic dis-
order."[27]

Wendell Glick provides the most logical answer to
the dilemma by stressing that Melville deplores with
Vere the injustice that finds Billy condemned.[28] Glick
argues that justice to the individual is not "the ultimate loyalty in a complex culture," according to Melville's story.[29] He states that "the stability of the
culture has a higher claim, and when the two conflict,
justice to the individual must be abrogated to keep the
order of society intact."[30]

The stress placed by Glick upon social expediency
argues for a weakness in individual morality. Adam,
David, and Isaac must all submit to corruption or be de-
stroyed by the Claggarts in society. Individuals like
Vere must make moral judgments when innocence and corruption collide. The price of this social expediency,
implies Glick, is a blighting, human mediocrity.[31]

Billy Budd, forced to leave the Rights-of-Man, went
aboard the Bellipotent where law, not morality, is su-

Note the use of
"op. cit." in foot-
note 27. The author
directs the reader
to Braswell's
original article
(footnote 25), not
to Stafford's case-
book (see "op. cit.,"
p. 116).

Footnote 31 re-
quires no "p." be-
cause the original
note, 28, requires
none (see p. 108).

[27]Braswell, op. cit., 143.

[28]"Expediency and Absolute Morality in Billy Budd,"
PMLA, 68 (March 1953), 104.

[29]Ibid.

[30]Ibid.

[31]Ibid., 105.

12

preme. His death is an image of the crucifixion, but
the image is not one of hope. William Braswell best
summarizes the mystery of the novel by suggesting that
the crucifixion, for Melville, "had long been an image
of human life, more suggestive of man's suffering than
of man's hope."[32]

[32]Braswell, 146.

There is no need to
carry the final foot-
note to the bottom
of the page. It
should immediately
follow the text.

Page number
omitted because of
major heading;
subsequent bibli-
ography pages
should be num-
bered in upper
right-hand corner.

Your instructor
may request that
you double space
entries in the
bibliography.

A Selected Bibliography

Arvin, Newton. Herman Melville: A Critical Biography.
     1950; rpt. New York: Compass-Viking, 1957.

Braswell, William. "Melville's Billy Budd as 'An Inside
     Narrative.'" American Literature, 29 (May 1957),
     133-46.

Glick, Wendell. "Expediency and Absolute Morality in
     Billy Budd." PMLA, 68 (March 1953), 103-10.

Lewis, Richard W. B. The American Adam: Innocence,
     Tragedy, and Tradition in the Nineteenth Century.
     Chicago: Univ. of Chicago Press, 1955.

Melville, Herman. Billy Budd, Sailor (An Inside Narra-
     tive). Ed. Harrison Hayford and Merton M. Sealts,
     Jr. Chicago: Univ. of Chicago Press, 1962.

Simpson, Cuthbert A. "Genesis." The Interpreter's
     Bible. 12 vols. Nashville: Abingdon, 1939.

Stafford, William T., ed. Billy Budd and the Critics.
     2nd ed. Belmont, Calif.: Wadsworth, 1968.

Watson, E. L. Grant. "Melville's Testament of Accep-
     tance." New England Quarterly, 6 (June 1933),
     319-27.

Weaver, Raymond M. "Introduction." The Shorter Novels
     of Herman Melville. 1928; rpt. New York: Premier-
     Fawcett, 1960.

Withim, Phil. "Billy Budd: Testament of Resistance."
     Modern Language Quarterly, 20 (June 1959), 115-
     27

Wright, Nathalia. Melville's Use of the Bible. Durham:
     Duke Univ. Press, 1949.

VI

FOOTNOTING

With as much effort as you have already exercised in organizing the body of your paper, you will now want to note your sources with complete accuracy. Consequently, you must credit in a footnote the source of every quotation, paraphrase, fact, or idea, specifying the exact location of each item so that the reader may investigate further if he so desires. Therefore, you should fully understand, perhaps even memorize, the basic forms of documentation — that is, both footnote and bibliography entries for a book and for a periodical article. (For a fuller discussion of bibliography entries, see pp. 117–30.)

The basic forms for a book are:

FOOTNOTE

     [1]Jon D. Longaker, <u>Art</u>, <u>Style</u>, <u>and History</u>
(Glenview, Ill.: Scott, Foresman, 1970), p. 39.

BIBLIOGRAPHY

    Longaker, Jon D. <u>Art</u>, <u>Style</u>, <u>and History</u>. Glenview,
       Ill.: Scott, Foresman, 1970.

In other words, a footnote for a book differs from the bibliography entry for that book in: indentation of the footnote, raised index numeral, author's given name first, a comma following his name, publication data within parentheses, and a specific page reference.

The basic forms for periodical articles are:

FOOTNOTE

     [1]Jesse Bier, "Weberism, Franklin, and the Transcen-
dental Style," <u>New England Quarterly</u>, 43 (June 1970), 180.

BIBLIOGRAPHY

    Bier, Jesse. "Weberism, Franklin, and the Transcendental
      Style." <u>New England Quarterly</u>, 43 (June 1970),
      179–92.

That is, a footnote for a periodical article differs from the bibliography entry for that article in: indentation of the footnote, raised index numeral, author's given name first, a comma following his name, a comma rather than a period following the title of the article, and a specific page reference rather than complete pagination.

You must keep your footnotes correct, clear, and concise. By recording data *carefully* and by double-checking each entry *before* typing the final manuscript, you can ensure accuracy. (Imagine the reaction of your reader, or instructor, if your reference directs him to page 568 of a book that contains only 364 pages!) Also, you must maintain clarity. Remember, for example, that "Ibid." should not appear as the first note on a page (thereby forcing the reader to turn back to the preceding page) and that "Smith, op. cit., p. 16" may confuse the reader more than a simple reference to "Smith, p. 16" (see p. 113). Finally, you should not interrupt the reader with numerous footnotes at the bottom of the page. In fact, in some cases, you can insert a brief note, within parentheses, in the text itself. Clearly, you will not seriously interrupt the reader's attention with such references in your text as (p. 35), (XI. 357), or (*Ham.* III.i.56–63). Remember, however, in such cases, to write a first full reference to a work that you cite often, putting it in proper footnote position at the bottom of the page, and saying therein that subsequent references to this edition appear in your text (see pp. 69–71).

When to Footnote

Sometimes the decision to document or not to document certain information with a footnote becomes troublesome. If in doubt, you should ask yourself, "Would a mature reader be likely to know this information?" If you believe he would not, you should provide a footnote that locates the source for the reader. For example, the fact that John F. Kennedy was president of the United States would not usually require a footnote entry. Nor would you probably need to indicate a source for the fact that Kennedy made the major decisions during the Cuban missile crisis. For that matter, his decision to effect a naval blockade of Cuba is common knowledge. However, you should credit, by means of a footnote, the source of specific decisions and statements by Kennedy—for example, his communications with Khrushchev, his cabinet decisions, or his public declarations.

Naturally, you will write into your paper ideas and concepts that you have assimilated in your own mind. These thoughts may be a combination of ideas suggested by the sources or they may be an original extension of an idea found in a source. In such cases, your thoughts cannot logically be credited to any one of your sources. Therefore, a good rule of thumb might well be the following: you should footnote when borrowing directly from your notes, but you may omit the footnote when you compose sentences not directly derived from reference material. Of course, you must always footnote a quotation, précis, summary, or paraphrased sentence. (See pp. 43–47, and the discussion of plagiarism, pp. 47–49.)

In addition, you may have a tendency to construct each paragraph so that a footnote at the end of it would blanket the entire unit. But this method may result in ambiguous references. Rather, you should consider each sentence you write as a separate unit, using the rule of thumb mentioned above to assess the general nature of the material contained in it. You should not find it necessary to footnote a complete paragraph if you synthesize and develop all the material as your own. (See "Handling Reference Material," pp. 64–73.)

Placing Footnote Numbers Within the Text

The rules for inserting footnote numbers into your text are:

1. Use Arabic numerals typed slightly above the line.
2. Always place the number at the *end* of your quotation, paraphrase, idea, and so on—not after introductory words or punctuation.
3. The footnote number comes immediately after the final word or punctuation—there is no space between a word or a mark of punctuation and the index numeral:

```
Melville also describes him as possessing an
amiable disposition, never giving offense to
anyone.5  And the author also says that Billy
"had none of that intuitive knowledge of the
bad. . . ."6
```

Arranging the Footnotes

When writing your footnotes, be sure to:

1. Number the footnotes consecutively throughout the entire paper (but by chapters in longer works).

2. Collect at the bottom of each page all footnotes for citations made on that page. (However, your instructor may request that you place all notes together on separate sheets at the end of your paper.)

3. Separate the footnotes from your text by triple spacing (that is, leave two lines of space). Also, single space each footnote, but double space between the notes:

```
without malice or deceitfulness.  He has no


     3E. L. Grant Watson, "Melville's Tes-
tament of Acceptance," New England Quarterly,
6 (June 1933), 320.


     4R. W. B. Lewis, The American Adam
(Chicago:  Univ. of Chicago Press, 1955),
p. 73.
```

(However, your instructor may request that you double space *all* materials, even the footnotes.)

4. Do not start a footnote on one page and complete it on the next. If you will count the number of line spaces required for your foot-note(s) on each page and if you make a soft pencil mark where your text should end and the footnotes begin, you will have no trouble with footnotes running off the bottom of the page. The technique is really quite simple: count the number of line spaces required for each note, add five line spaces for the one inch bottom margin, allow two line spaces to separate the text and the first footnote, and, finally, figure any line spaces to separate two or more footnotes. Thus, the three sample footnotes above would require fourteen line spaces.

5. Employ a separate line for each footnote unless you have numerous short notes. The following form is acceptable:

```
     4Johnson, p. 3.        6Thomas, p. 456.

     5Ibid., p. 9.         7Johnson, p. 9.
```

Also acceptable:

```
        4Johnson, p. 3.

        5Ibid., p. 9.

        6Thomas, p. 456.

        7Johnson, p. 9.
```

Footnote Form—Books

You should use the following order when placing data for books within the first, full footnote, omitting any unnecessary items:

1. The author's or authors' name(s), in normal order, followed by a comma:

```
    1John Seelye, Melville:  The Ironic Diagram
(Evanston, Ill.:  Northwestern Univ. Press, 1970),
pp. 96–97.
```

Avoid abbreviations by providing the name in the fullest form known to you. Imagine the dilemma of a reader searching the card catalog for "L. Lewis" or "J. H. Smith"! However, if you supply missing ingredients — that is, ones not given on the title page of the book — place them within square brackets (for example, "L[awrence] Lewis"). In the case of well known authors — for example, "T. S. Eliot" and "Dante" — give the name in its most usual form.

2. The title of the chapter or part of the book, within quotation marks, followed by a comma inside the final quotes:

```
    2Robert Penn Warren, "Blackberry Winter," Read-
ing Modern Short Stories, ed. Jarvis A. Thurston (Chi-
cago:  Scott, Foresman, 1955), p. 578.
```

This entry is usually necessary only with articles in collections or specific chapters of long reference works.

3. The title of the book, underlined, followed by a comma unless the next item is enclosed within parentheses:

```
    3Noel Stock, The Life of Ezra Pound (New York:
Pantheon, 1970), p. 225.
```

Use the full title as shown on the title page of the book, including any subtitle (which you distinguish by a colon).

4. The name of the editor, translator, or compiler, in normal order, preceded by "ed.," "trans.," or "comp.," followed by a comma unless the next item is enclosed within parentheses:

> [4]Olof Lagercrantz, From Hell to Paradise: Dante and His Comedy, trans. Alan Blair (New York: Washington Square Press, 1966), p. 20.

If you are discussing the editor's or translator's work rather than the text, provide his name first, followed by a comma, followed by "ed." or "trans." and another comma. Place the author's name, if any, preceded with a comma and "by," after the title:

> [5]Hazelton Spencer, ed., Elizabethan Plays (Boston: Little, Brown, 1933), p. 102.

> [6]Richard Lattimore, trans., The Iliad, by Homer (Chicago: Univ. of Chicago Press, 1962), p. iii.

5. The edition number, if it is not the first, in Arabic numerals, followed by a comma unless the next item is enclosed within parentheses:

> [7]May Hill Arbuthnot, Children and Books, 3rd ed. (Chicago: Scott, Foresman, 1964), p. 16.

Reprints of texts, paperbacks especially, require notation of the original date and edition as well as publication facts of the reprint [[7]John Livingston Lowes, *The Road to Xanadu: A Study in the Ways of the Imagination*, 2nd ed. (1930; rpt. New York: Vintage-Knopf, 1959), p. 76.].

6. The series name, without quotation marks and not underlined, followed by a comma, followed by the number of this book in the series, followed by a comma unless the next item is enclosed within parentheses:

> [8]David Fowler, Piers the Plowman, Univ. of Washington Publications in Lang. and Lit., 16 (Seattle: Univ. of Washington Press, 1961), p. 89.

7. The number of volumes with this title, in Arabic numerals (for example "5 vols."). Use only if there is more than one volume and the information is pertinent—that is, if your reference is to the work as a whole, not to a specific passage:

> [9]Vernon L. Parrington, Main Currents in American Thought, 3 vols. (New York: Harcourt, Brace, 1927–32).

Note the omission of a page number in this footnote because the reference is to the entire work.

8. The place, publisher, and date of publication within parentheses and with a colon between the place and publisher and commas after the publisher and the second parenthesis:

> [10]Andrew Wright, <u>A Reader's Guide to English and American Literature</u> (Glenview, Ill.: Scott, Foresman, 1970), p. xix.

If more than one city appears on the title page, use only the first. Include the name of the state if necessary for clarity (for example, "Springfield, Mass." or "Springfield, Ill."). Exclude the name of the publisher only if your instructor so stipulates. If the title page does not carry the publication date, use the most recent copyright date as shown on the reverse side of the title page.

9. The volume number, if the book is one of two or more volumes with the same title, in Roman numerals, followed by a comma:

> [11]Edgar Allan Poe, "MS. Found in a Bottle," <u>The Works of Edgar Allan Poe</u> (New York: Crowell, 1902), II, 1–15.

If the volumes were published in different years, show this fact by placing the volume number *before* the place and date of publication:

> [12]Vernon L. Parrington, "Roger Williams," <u>Main Currents in American Thought</u>, I (New York: Harcourt, Brace, 1927), 62.

10. Page number(s), preceded by a comma, in Arabic numerals unless the text has small Roman numerals (for example, "p. iv."). Use "p." and "pp." only for works of a single volume. Also note the following common usage: "pp. 92–93," not "pp. 92–3"; but "pp. 215–18," not "pp. 215–8" or "pp. 215–218." Page numbers are followed by a period unless some additional information must be included (for example, "p. 12, n. 2.").

SPECIMEN FOOTNOTES – BOOKS

Author, *first full reference*

> [1]John Seelye, <u>Melville</u>: <u>The Ironic Diagram</u> (Evanston, Ill.: Northwestern Univ. Press, 1970), pp. 96–97.

Author's name already given in text

> [1]<u>Melville</u>: <u>The Ironic Diagram</u> (Evanston, Ill.: Northwestern Univ. Press, 1970), pp. 96–97.
> Use this form even if both author and title are given in your text.

Author, *anonymous*

    [2]The Song of Roland, trans. Frederick Bliss Lu-
quines (New York: Macmillan, 1960), p. 22.

Author, *anonymous but name supplied*

    [3][James Madison], All Impressments Unlawful and In-
admissible (Boston: William Pelham, 1804), p. 10.

Author, *pseudonymous but name supplied*

    [4]Robert Slender [Philip Freneau], Letters on Various
and Important Subjects (Philadelphia: D. Hogan, 1799),
p. 140.

Authors, *two*

    [5]Vivian Edmonston Todd and Helen Heffernan, The
Years Before School: Guiding Preschool Children, 2nd
ed. (New York: Macmillan, 1970), p. 357.

Authors, *three*

    [6]Wilbur O. Sypherd, A. M. Fountain, and V. E. Gib-
bens, Manual of Technical Writing (Chicago: Scott,
Foresman, 1957), p. 60.

Authors, *more than three*

    [7]Albert C. Baugh et al., A Literary History of En-
gland, 2nd ed. (New York: Appleton, 1967), p. 797.

The use of "and others" (see p. 116) is also acceptable.

Classical works

    [8]Homer, The Iliad, trans. Richard Lattimore (Chi-
cago: Univ. of Chicago Press, 1951), p. 101 (Bk. III,
ll. 38–45).

    [9]Plato, The Republic, trans. Paul Shorey (Cam-
bridge, Mass.: Harvard Univ. Press, 1937), p. 225
(III, vi).

You should give the reader more information than the page number
for classics that appear in several editions. However, do not use this
form if you make numerous citations to one work. Rather, you
should provide an initial full reference and thereafter place the documentation in your text (see pp. 70–72).

Component part of a book

    [10]Robert Browning, "My Last Duchess," Better Read-
ing Two: Literature, ed. Walter Blair. John Gerber, and
Eugene Garber, 4th ed. (Chicago: Scott, Foresman, 1966),
pp. 55–56.

    [11]Flannery O'Connor, "The Nature and Aim of Fic-
tion," Mystery and Manners, by Flannery O'Connor, ed.
Sally and Robert Fitzgerald (New York: Noonday, 1970),
pp. 76–77.

Corporate authorship

[12]Committee on Telecommunications, <u>Reports</u> <u>on</u> <u>Selected</u> <u>Topics</u> <u>in</u> <u>Telecommunications</u> (New York: National Academy of Sciences, National Research Council, 1970), p. 4.

Edition

[13]Oscar Thompson, <u>The</u> <u>International</u> <u>Cyclopedia</u> <u>of</u> <u>Music</u> <u>and</u> <u>Musicians</u>, rev. Robert Sabin, 9th ed. (New York: Dodd, Mead, 1964), p. 81.

Editor

[14]Hugh Henry Brackenridge, <u>Modern</u> <u>Chivalry</u>, ed. Claude M. Newlin (New York: American Book, 1962), p. 18.

The writer is citing Brackenridge, the author.

[15]Hardin Craig, ed., <u>The</u> <u>Complete</u> <u>Works</u> <u>of</u> <u>Shake-</u><u>speare</u>, rev. ed. (Chicago: Scott, Foresman, 1961), p. 22.

The writer is citing Craig, the editor.

Encyclopedia

[16]Inga-Stina Ewbank, "Dickens," <u>Encyclopedia</u> <u>Americana</u>, 1970.

Footnotes to unsigned articles begin with the title of the article. Authors of encyclopedia articles are usually identified by initials at the end of the article and by an accompanying index to the initials in the front of each volume. References alphabetically arranged need not be identified by volume and page.

Introduction

[17]Arnold J. Toynbee, "Introduction," <u>The</u> <u>Great</u> <u>Frontier</u>, by Walter Prescott Webb (Austin, Texas: Univ. of Texas Press, 1964). p. ix.

Manuscript collections

[18]British Museum, <u>Cotton</u> <u>Vitellius</u>, A. XV.

[19]Corpus Christi College, Cambridge, MS CCCC 201.

Play, *classical*

[20]Sophocles, <u>Oedipus</u> <u>the</u> <u>King</u>, in <u>The</u> <u>Complete</u> <u>Greek</u> <u>Tragedies</u>, ed. David Grene and Richard Lattimore (Chicago: Univ. of Chicago Press, 1959), II, 52 (ll. 977-83).

[21]William Shakespeare, <u>Macbeth</u>, in <u>Shakespeare:</u> <u>Twenty-Three</u> <u>Plays</u> <u>and</u> <u>the</u> <u>Sonnets</u>, ed. T. M. Parrott (New York: Scribner's, 1953), p. 835 (II.i.33-43).

Play, *modern*

[22]Tom Stoppard, <u>Rosencrantz</u> <u>and</u> <u>Guildenstern</u> <u>Are</u> <u>Dead</u> (New York: Grove Press, 1967), p. 16.

[23]Graham Greene, <u>The</u> <u>Complaisant</u> <u>Lover</u> (New York: Viking Press, 1959), p. 52 (I.ii).

Here again, you may wish to give the reader additional information, but it is seldom necessary with modern works.

Poem, *classical*

[24]Dante, "Purgatorio," <u>The</u> <u>Divine</u> <u>Comedy</u>, trans. Lawrence Grant White (New York: Pantheon, 1948), p. 74 (vii.1–12).

[25]Edmund Spenser, <u>The</u> <u>Faerie</u> <u>Queen</u>, ed. Ernest Rhys (London: Dutton, 1910), I, 58–59 (I.iv.21).

Note that this edition of *The Faerie Queen* is published in two volumes.

Poem, *modern*

[26]Robert Penn Warren, "Holly and Hickory," <u>You</u>, <u>Emperors</u>, <u>and</u> <u>Others</u>: <u>Poems</u> <u>1957</u>–<u>1960</u> (New York: Random House, 1960), p. 38.

[27]John Keats, "Ode to a Nightingale," <u>Beginnings</u> <u>in</u> <u>Poetry</u>, ed. William J. Martz (Chicago: Scott, Foresman, 1965), pp. 90–92.

Reprint

[28]Raymond M. Weaver, "Introduction," <u>The</u> <u>Shorter</u> <u>Novels</u> <u>of</u> <u>Herman</u> <u>Melville</u> (1928; rpt. New York: Premier–Fawcett, 1960), p. 56.

Series, *numbered*

[29]David Fowler, <u>Piers</u> <u>the</u> <u>Plowman</u>, Univ. of Washington Publications in Lang. and Lit., 16 (Seattle: Univ. of Washington Press, 1961), p. 89.

Since a series number rather than a volume number is given, use the abbreviation "p."

Series, *unnumbered*

[30]Lawrence Henry Gibson, <u>The</u> <u>Coming</u> <u>of</u> <u>the</u> <u>Revolu</u>–<u>tion</u>: <u>1762</u>–<u>1775</u>, ed. Henry Steele Commager and Richard B. Morris, The New American Nation Series (New York: Harper, 1954), pp. 1–10.

[31]Howard E. Wilson, "Education, Foreign Policy, and International Affairs," <u>Cultural</u> <u>Affairs</u> <u>and</u> <u>Foreign</u> <u>Relations</u>, ed. Robert Blum, The American Assembly Series (Englewood Cliffs, N. J.: Prentice–Hall, 1963), p. 22.

Translator

[32]Olof Lagercrantz, <u>From</u> <u>Hell</u> <u>to</u> <u>Paradise</u>: <u>Dante</u> <u>and</u> <u>His</u> <u>Comedy</u>, trans. Alan Blair (New York: Washington Square Press, 1966), p. 20.

The writer is citing Lagercrantz, the author.

³³Richard Lattimore, trans., The Iliad, by Homer (Chicago: Univ. of Chicago Press, 1962), p. iii.

> The writer is citing Lattimore, the translator.

Volumes, *one of several*

³⁴Edgar Allan Poe, "MS. Found in a Bottle," The Works of Edgar Allan Poe (New York: Crowell, 1902), II, 1–15.

> If all volumes were published in the same year, place the volume number after the facts of publication.

³⁵Christopher Marlowe, The Tragical History of Doctor Faustus, in The Literature of England, ed. George K. Anderson and William E. Buckler, 5th ed. (Chicago: Scott, Foresman, 1966), I, 711.

> Since *The Tragical History of Doctor Faustus* is italicized, you may introduce the collection in which it appears with the word "in."

³⁶Harold Child, "Jane Austen," The Cambridge History of English Literature, ed. A. W. Ward and A. R. Waller, XII (London: Cambridge Univ. Press, 1914), 231–33.

> Since the volumes of this work were published in different years, the volume number precedes the facts of publication. Compare notes 37 and 38.

³⁷Vernon L. Parrington, "Roger Williams," Main Currents in American Thought, I (New York: Harcourt, Brace, 1927), 62.

³⁸Bliss Perry, The American Spirit in Literature, in The Chronicles of America Series, ed. Allen Johnson, XXXIV (New Haven: Yale Univ. Press, 1918), 35.

> Since *The American Spirit in Literature* is an entire volume, italics may be used.

Works alphabetically arranged

³⁹Edmund K. Alden, "Alden, John," DAB (1928).

> This note to a familiar biographical dictionary, alphabetically arranged, eliminates the need for a long, possibly confusing reference to *The Dictionary of American Biography*, ed. Allen Johnson (New York: Scribner's, 1928), I, 146–47.

Footnote Form — Periodicals

You should use the following order when placing data within the first, full footnote, omitting any items that are unnecessary:

1. The author's name, in normal order, followed by a comma:

¹Jesse Bier, "Weberism, Franklin, and the Transcendental Style," New England Quarterly, 43 (June 1970), 180.

2. The complete title of the article, enclosed within quotation marks, followed by a comma inside the second quotation mark (see footnote 1 above).

3. The name of the periodical, underlined, followed by a comma (see footnote 1 above).

4. The volume number (without the abbreviation "Vol." preceding), in Arabic numerals, followed by a comma unless the next item is enclosed within parentheses (see footnote 1 above). However, omit the volume number for weekly or monthly periodicals which are paged anew in each issue. Give instead the complete date, set off by commas, not parentheses:

> [2]Benjamin DeMott, "Saul Bellow and the Dogmas of Possibility," <u>Saturday Review</u>, 7 Feb. 1970, pp. 25–26.

5. The issue number or name of the issue (for example, "Spring") only when pagination of the issue is separate and the month of publication is not given:

> [3]William R. Elkins, "Thoreau's <u>Cape Cod</u>: The Violent Pond," <u>Oklahoma English Bulletin</u>, 2, No. 2 (1965), 15.

or

> [3]William R. Elkins, "Thoreau's <u>Cape Cod</u>: The Violent Pond," <u>Oklahoma English Bulletin</u>, 2 (Fall 1965), 15.

6. The month (if needed) and year, enclosed in parentheses, followed by a comma. If you can quickly determine that all issues of a journal fall within a calendar year, use only the year. You must always precede the year with the month or season (Spring 1970) when pagination is separate in the issues of a magazine. When in doubt, include the month.

> [4]Hans Joachim Marx, "Some Corelli Attributions Assessed," <u>Musical Quarterly</u>, 56 (1970), 89.

> [5]James E. Miller, Jr., "The Linguistic Imagination," <u>College English</u>, 31 (April 1970), 727.

7. The page number(s), in Arabic numerals, followed by a period, except when additional information follows (for example, "17, n."). Use the abbreviations "p." or "pp." only when a volume number is *not* included in the reference:

[6]Harry T. Moore, "Motes in the Eye of a Mountainous Man," Saturday Review, 7 March 1970, pp. 23–24.

Since a volume number is *not* included, use the abbreviation "pp."

[7]Robert M. Jordan, "The Non–Dramatic Disunity of the Merchant's Tale," PMLA, 78 (Sept. 1963), 293–94.

Since a volume number is provided, do *not* use the abbreviation "pp."

SPECIMEN FOOTNOTES — PERIODICALS

[1]John A. Dussinger, "Conscience and the Pattern of Christian Perfection in Clarissa," PMLA, 81 (June 1966), 238–39.

[2]Allen Austin, "T. S. Eliot's Theory of Personal Expression," PMLA, 81 (June 1966), 303, n. 3.

[3]Raven I. McDavid, "Sense and Nonsense About American Dialects," PMLA, 81, No. 2 (1966), 9–11.

The issue number is provided because this issue is paged separately although it appears in the same volume of *PMLA* as the first two references.

[4]Dean T. Mace, "Pietro Bembo and the Literary Origins of the Italian Madrigal," Musical Quarterly, 55 (Jan. 1969), 66.

[5]Brom Weber, rev. of The World of Flannery O'Connor, by Josephine Hendin, Saturday Review, 18 July 1970, p. 29.

Note the differences in the form for a weekly periodical.

[6]Ruth Kilchenmann, "Traum und Wirklichkeit in den Werken Friedrich Schnacks," German Quarterly, 34 (May 1961), 260–62.

[7]Leonard Cottrell, "How Egypt Lived and Died," Réalités, March 1970, pp. 52–53.

Use this form for a monthly periodical that is paged separately.

[8]Mary Mothersill, "Moral Knowledge," Journal of Philosophy, 56 (10 Sept. 1959), 755–56.

Since this journal is published fortnightly, yet is paged continuously through each volume, a more specific date is provided.

[9]Warren Bennett, "Character, Irony, and Resolution in 'A Clean, Well–Lighted Place,'" American Literature, 62 (March 1970), 70–71, 74.

This page reference is clearer to the reader than "70ff."

[10]Frank H. Sommer, "The Iconography of Action: Bernini's Ludovica Albertone," Art Quarterly, 33 (1970), 31.

Write "(Spring 1970)" if you cannot quickly determine that this journal's four issues fall within the calendar year.

[11]Charlton Ogburn, Jr., "The Motorcar vs. America," American Heritage, 21, No. 4 (June 1970), 104.

Footnote Form — Public Documents

Since the nature of public documents is so varied, the form of the entry cannot be standardized. Therefore, common sense tells you to provide sufficient information so that the reader can easily locate the reference. Note the following:

[1]U.S., Bureau of the Budget, Special Analysis: Budget of the United States, Fiscal year 1967 (Washington, D.C.: GPO, 1966), p. 2

[2]Higher Education Act of 1965, 79 Stat. (1965).

Compare *Swain v. Alabama* below. Court cases and legislative acts follow a form stipulated by law publications. The act or case is listed first, followed by the volume number, abbreviated title, and date of the work in which the act or case is found. Also, notice that the volume number is in Arabic numerals, that the date is placed within parentheses, and that a court case is italized but an act is not.

[3]Swain v. Alabama, 380 U.S. (1965).

[4]U.S., Congress, Senate, Senate Joint Resolution 1, 89th Cong., 1st sess., 1965, pp. 2–3.

[5]U.S., Congressional Record, 88th Cong., 2nd sess., 1964, CX, Part 18, 23504–05.

[6]U.S., Constitution, Art. 2, sec. 1.

[7]U.S., Department of State, Foreign Relations of the United States: Diplomatic Papers, 1943, II, 175–77.

Compare footnote 8 below. Since the date is part of the title, it precedes the volume number.

[8]U.S., Department of State, United States Treaties and Other International Agreements, XV, Part 1, 1964, 556.

[9]U.S., Congress, House, Committee on Interstate and Foreign Commerce, Federal Cigarette Labeling and Advertising Act, 89th Cong., 1st sess., 1965, H. Rept. 449 to accompany H. R. 3014, pp. 9–12.

[10]U.S., President, "John F. Kennedy: 1963," Public Papers of the Presidents of the United States (Washington, D.C.: Office of the Federal Registrar, 1964), pp. 454–55.

[11]U.S., Congress, Senate, Committee on Foreign Relations, Hearings on S. 2793, Supplemental Foreign Assistance Fiscal Year 1966—Vietnam, 89th Cong., 2nd sess., 1966, p. 8.

[12]U.S., Congress, Senate, The Constitution of the United States of America: Analysis and Interpretation, Senate Document 170, 82nd Cong., 2nd sess., 1952, pp. 512–13.

[13]U.S., Statutes at Large, LXXII, Part 1, 455.

[14]Kansas, Session Laws 1963, pp. 601–06.

Footnote Form — Other Sources

The sample entries below will enable you to determine a suitable footnote form for other types of reference material:

Bulletin

     [1]Earl French, "Personal Problems in Industrial Research and Development," Bulletin of N.Y. State School of Industrial and Labor Relations, No. 51 (Oct. 1963), p. 22.

Dissertation, *published*

     [2]Per Nykrog, <u>Les Fabliaux</u>: <u>Etude d'histoire littéraire et de stylistique médiévale</u>, Diss. Aarhus 1957 (Copenhagen: Munksgaard, 1957), p. 62.

Dissertation, *unpublished*

     [3]Emmett Loy Phillips, "A Study of Aesthetic Distance in Thoreau's <u>Walden</u>," Diss. Univ. of Oklahoma 1970, p. 42.

     [4]Emmett Loy Phillips, "A Study of Aesthetic Distance in Thoreau's <u>Walden</u>," <u>Dissertation Abstracts International</u>, 30 (1970), 3953–A (Univ. of Oklahoma).

    A note to the abstract, not the dissertation itself.

Interview

     [5]Interview with Bill Rayson, Director, Credit Bureau, Tulsa, Oklahoma, May 2, 1970.

Lecture

     [6]Charles C. Jones, "Thomas Jefferson," Lecture presented at Kansas State Teachers College, Emporia, Kansas, July 6, 1965.

    See also "Public Address," p. 112.

Letter, *personal*

     [7]Information in a letter to the author from Professor David S. Berkeley of Oklahoma State University, March 6, 1966.

Mimeographed material

     [8]Jane Smith, "Terms for the Study of Fiction" (mimeographed paper, Cleveland, 1970), p. 2.

Monograph

     [9]NEA Research Division, <u>Kindergarten Practices, 1961</u> (monograph 1962–M2, Washington, D.C., 1962), p. 3.

     [10]William R. Veeder, <u>W. B. Yeats</u>: <u>The Rhetoric of Repetition</u>, Univ. of California English Studies, 34 (Berkeley, Univ. of California Press, 1968), p. 12.

Newspaper

[11]John Peterson, "Assault on Heart Disease," National Observer, 20 July 1970, p. 1, cols. 4–5, and p. 17, cols. 1–6.

[12]Editorial, "The Irregular Intellectuals," National Observer, 20 July 1970, p. 10.

Pamphlet

[13]U. S. Civil Service Commission, The Human Equation: Working in Personnel for the Federal Government, Pamphlet 76 (Washington, D. C.: GPO, May 1970), pp. 2–4.

Public address

[14]David Sarnoff, "Television: A Channel for Freedom," Address presented at the University of Detroit Academic Convocation, Detroit, 1961.

See also "Lecture," p. 111.

Recording

[15]"Chaucer: The Nun's Priest's Tale," Caedmon recording, No. E8C40. Narrated in Middle English by Robert Ross.

[16]"I Can Hear It Now: Winston Churchill," ed. Edward R. Murrow and Fred W. Friendly, Columbia Masterworks recording, No. E9C10. Narrator, Edward R. Murrow.

Report

[17]Thomas Huber, "U. S. Study Programs and West German Educational Institutions: A Report on Problems and Prospects" (New York: Institute of International Education, 1969), pp. 2–4.

[18]Panama Canal Company, Annual Report: Fiscal Year Ended June 30, 1968 (Panama: Canal Zone Government, 1968), pp. 7–9.

Source Books

Source books contain articles gathered from other publications and compiled into one book. These act, therefore, as a small library. If possible, you should find the original material, cite from it, and document accordingly. But when you cannot locate the primary source, cite from your source book and use the following method of footnote documentation:

[19] Cleanth Brooks, "The Formalist Critics," Kenyon Review, 13 (1951), 73, rpt. in H. G. Duffield and Manuel Bilsky, eds., Tolstoy and the Critics: Literature and Aesthetics (Chicago: Scott, Foresman, 1965), p. 13.

In other words, you provide an exact reference to both books, including page numbers.

[20]Richard Ellmann, "Reality," Yeats: The Man and the Masks (New York: Macmillan, 1948), rpt. in John Unterecker, ed., Yeats: A Collection of Critical Essays, Twentieth Century Views (Englewood Cliffs, N. J.: Prentice-Hall, 1963), p. 165.

> In this instance, the source book does not provide pagination of the original; therefore, you must omit a page reference to Ellmann's book and supply a page reference to the source book only.

Television or radio program

[21]"Town Meeting of the World," C.B.S. telecast, March 1, 1966: "Nuclear Proliferation." Narrator, Eric Sevareid.

Thesis, *published*

See "Dissertation, published," p. 111.

Thesis, *unpublished*

See "Dissertation, unpublished," p. 111.

Unpublished paper

[23]William R. Elkins, "The Dream World and the Dream Vision: Meaning and Structure in Poe's Art," an unpublished paper.

Subsequent References

After you once provide full reference data for a primary citation, your subsequent notes for the same source should be brief but clear. Normally, the author's last name and the page number will suffice (for example, "Johnson, p. 12."). However, if the full first reference is not found in a recent note or if you are citing more than one book by this author, you should add the title, preferably in the shortest possible form (for example, "Johnson, *Experiences,* p. 12."). If another author has an identical surname, you must add the given name to each reference (for example, "James Johnson, p. 12.").

As an alternative to repeating the title or author's name, you may use the Latinate abbreviation "Ibid." ('in the same place') *if* it refers to the source in the immediately preceding footnote and *if* it appears on the same page.[1] For example, when you refer to the identical page(s) of the preceding note, insert only "Ibid.," capitalized and followed by a period ("Ibid."). If your reference is to the same book as the preceding note but to a different page, insert "Ibid.," followed by a comma, followed by the page number ("Ibid., p. 16.").

[1]The *MLA Style Sheet* considers "Ibid." and other Latinate words as Americanized, thereby negating the need for underlining. Your professor, however, may desire that you underline the Latinate words.

You should find it unnecessary to employ the Latinate abbreviations "op. cit." and "loc. cit." "Op. cit." is an abbreviation for *opere citato,* which means 'in the work cited.' It is sometimes employed when nonconsecutive references are made to the same work (for example, "Jones, op. cit., p. 65."). But a simple reference to "Jones, p. 65" serves the same purpose and is less confusing. "Loc. cit." is an abbreviation for *loco citato,* which means 'in the place cited.' Since this footnote names the exact source listed immediately preceding it, the author's name and a page reference are omitted (for example, "Loc. cit."). But the use of "Ibid." without a page reference serves the same purpose (see above).

Note the following sequence of specimen footnotes:

[1]Noel Stock, The Life of Ezra Pound (New York: Pantheon, 1970), pp. 33–34.

[2]Ibid., p. 35.

But do not use this form if it occurs on a different page.

[3]Laurence Perrine, Sound and Sense: An Introduction to Poetry (New York: Harcourt, Brace & World, 1963), p. 45.

[4]The Castle (New York: Knopf, 1954), p. 412.

Use this form when the author's name and even the title have been given in the text.

[5]Perrine, p. 12.

[6]Stock, p. 36.

[7]Frederick J. Hoffman, The Achievement of Randall Jarrell (Glenview, Ill.: Scott, Foresman, 1970), p. 7.

[8]Ibid.

But use only on the same page with footnote 7.

[9]Ibid., p. 29.

But use only on the same page with footnotes 7 and 8.

[10]Laurence Perrine, Story and Structure, 2nd ed. (New York: Harcourt, Brace & World, 1966), p. 4.

[11]Wendell Glick, "Expediency and Absolute Morality in Billy Budd," PMLA, 68 (March 1953), 104.

[12]Perrine, Sound and Sense, p. 124.

Since two books by Perrine appear above, you must add a title to this note.

[13]Glick, 104; cf. William Braswell, "Melville's Billy Budd as 'An Inside Narrative,'" American Literature, 29 (May 1957), 133–46.

[14]Glick, 108.

"Ibid., 108" would, perhaps, confuse the reader.

15Kafka, The Castle, p. 406.
If this note appears several pages beyond footnote 4, you extend common courtesy by providing both author and title.

16James E. Miller, Jr., "The Linguistic Imagination," College English, 31 (April 1970), 727.

17Ibid., 728; cf. Glick, "Expediency," 105.

18See, e.g., Allen Austin, "T. S. Eliot's Theory of Personal Expression," PMLA, 81 (June 1966), 303.

19Kafka, pp. 409–10.

Content Footnotes

As shown on the preceding pages, reference footnotes perform the basic function of documenting the original source. But you may have occasion to write other types of notes, classified as content footnotes, offering further information that the average reader might need or profit by. Rather than distract the reader with an incidentally related item within the text, you should place it within a footnote, using one of the following types of brief content footnotes:

Definition

1Briefly, existentialism expounds the theory that man lives in a purposeless universe in which he must exercise freedom of will to combat his environment.
This type of note defines or amplifies a term or phrase you have used in the text.

Explanation and Elaboration

2Jean–Paul Sartre became the chief spokesman for existentialism in France after World War II. (Smith, p. 6.)
This note offers additional information that is not pertinent to textual matters. The entry at the end is necessary if the information is borrowed from an authority.

Evaluation and Comparison of Authorities

3Cf. Edmund Wilson, Axel's Castle, p. 114: "As a critic, Eliot occupies today a position of distinction and influence equal in importance to his position as a poet."
The writer is asking the reader to compare textual analysis with Wilson's statement.

Cross Reference to Another Part of the Paper

4The importance of Emerson as a poet, however, is questioned by some authorities. See above, p. 3.
The writer is asking the reader to refer to an earlier portion of the paper for the discussion of Emerson.

Abbreviations in Footnotes

You should employ abbreviations often and consistently in the footnotes, though in your text you should avoid them (except "Dr.," "Esq.," "Hon.," "Jr.," "Mr.," "Mrs.," "Rev.," and "St."). In footnotes you should abbreviate dates (for example, "Jan.," "Feb.") and institutions (for example "Univ.," "Assn."). Finally, you may use or encounter the following common abbreviations and reference words:

A.D. *anno Domini* 'in the year of the Lord'; precedes numerals with no space between letters, as in "A.D. 350"

anon. anonymous

art., arts. article(s)

B.C. 'Before Christ'; follows numerals with no space between letters, as in "500 B.C."

bk., bks. book(s)

ca. (or c.) *circa* 'about,' used to indicate an approximate date, as in "ca. 1812"

cf. *confer* 'compare' (one source with another); not, however, to be used in place of "see"

ch., chs. (or chap., chaps.) chapter(s)

col., cols. column(s)

comp. compiled (by) or compiler

diss. dissertation

ed., eds. editor(s), edition, or edited (by)

e.g. *exempli gratia* 'for example,' preceded and followed by a comma

enl. enlarged, as in "enl. ed."

esp. especially, as in "pp. 312–15, esp. p. 313"

et al. *et alii* 'and others'; "John Smith et al." means John Smith and other authors

et pas. *et passim* 'and here and there' (see "passim")

et seq. *et sequens* 'and the following'; "pp. 9 et seq.' means page nine and the following page; compare "f." and "ff."

f., ff. page or pages following a given page; "pp. 8 f." means page eight and the following page; but exact references are preferable, for example, "pp. 45–51, 55, 58" instead of "pp. 45 ff."

ibid. *ibidem* 'in the same place,' i.e., in the immediately preceding title (see p. 113).

i.e. *id est* 'that is,' preceded and followed by a comma

illus. illustrated by, illustrations, or illustrator

infra 'below,' refers to a succeeding portion of the text; compare "supra." Generally, it is best to write "see below"

intro. (or introd.) introduction (by)

l., ll. line(s)

loc. cit. *loco citato* 'in the place (passage) cited' (see p. 114)

MS, MSS manuscript(s); but followed by a period ("MS.") when referring to a specific manuscript

n., nn. note(s), as "p. 23, n. 2" or "p. 51 n."

n.d. no date (in a book's title or copyright pages)

no., nos. number(s)

n.p. no place (of publication)

op. cit. *opere citato* 'in the work cited' (see p. 114)

p., pp. page(s); use "Pages" instead of "Pp."

passim 'here and there throughout the work,' e.g., "pp. 67, 72, et passim"

pseud. pseudonym

pt., pts. part(s)

rev. revised (by), revision, review, or reviewed (by)

rpt. reprint, reprinted

sec., secs. section(s)

sic 'thus,' placed in brackets to indicate an error has been made in the quoted passage and the writer is quoting accurately

st., sts. stanza(s)

sup. (or supra) 'above,' refers to a preceding portion of the text; it is just as easy to write "above"

s.v. *sub voce (verbo)* 'under the word or heading'

trans. (or tr.) translator, translated (by), or translation

vol., vols. volume(s), as in "Vol. III"

VII

THE BIBLIOGRAPHY

After writing your paper, you should prepare a selected bibliography, listing only the source material actually used in the writing of your manuscript. That is, you should provide publication data for each reference. In fact, some instructors may request that you label the bibliography "List of References Cited." In other words, the bibliography will offer the reader a limited indication of the scholarship related to your subject.

If you have carefully developed your working bibliography (pp. 9–14), you will find that preparation of the final one is a relatively simple process. In fact, the final bibliography is not a new assignment because your bibliography cards, arranged alphabetically, already provide the necessary information. However, this fact will be true only if you have kept the bibliography cards up-to-date during note-taking by adding new sources and by disposing of cards that you have found to be irrelevant.

To repeat: you should include in the bibliography all works actually used in your study. And you must, without exception, include a bibliography entry for all first references in the footnotes. You may also insert other works pertinent to the paper, but do not include books that were of no value in the research, even though you investigated them.

Bibliography Form

You should arrange the items of the bibliography in alphabetical order by the surname of the author. Place the first line of each entry flush with the left margin and indent succeeding lines approximately five spaces. Single space each entry, but double space between each reference. (However, your instructor may request that you double space all materials, even the individual bibliography entries.) Study carefully the examples given in the following sample "Selected Bibliography":

A SELECTED BIBLIOGRAPHY

Catford, J. C. "Phonology and the Teaching of
    Pronunciation." <u>College English</u>, 27 (May
    1966), 605-13.

Ciardi, John, trans. <u>The Purgatorio</u>, by Dante.
    New York: New American Library, 1961.

Cohen, B. Bernard. <u>Literature for Understanding</u>.
    Chicago: Scott, Foresman, 1966.

------------. <u>Writing About Literature</u>. Chicago:
    Scott, Foresman, 1963.

Lagercrantz, Olof. <u>From Hell to Paradise</u>: <u>Dante
    and His Comedy</u>. Trans. Alan Blair. New York:
    Washington Square Press, 1966.

Parrington, Vernon L. <u>Main Currents in American
    Thought</u>. 3 vols. New York: Harcourt, Brace,
    1927-32.

Weaver, Raymond. "Introduction." <u>The Shorter Novels
    of Herman Melville</u>. 1928; rpt. New York:
    Premier-Fawcett, 1960.

Woodson, Thomas. "Thoreau on Poverty and Magna-
    nimity." <u>PMLA</u>, 85 (Jan. 1970), 21-34.

**Fig.39: Sample
Bibliography Page**

BIBLIOGRAPHY FORM—BOOKS

When entering references to books, you should use the following order, omitting unnecessary items:

1. The author's name, surname first, followed by given name or initials, followed by a period:

Seelye, John. <u>Melville</u>: <u>The Ironic Diagram</u>. Evanston,
    Ill.: Northwestern Univ. Press, 1970.

Always give authors' names in the fullest possible form; for example, "Cosbey, Robert C." rather than "Cosbey, R. C." unless, as indicated on the title page of the book, the author's preference is for initials.

However, if an author has two or more works in the bibliography, do not repeat his name with each work. Rather, insert a continuous, twelve-space line flush with the left margin, followed by a period:

Perrine, Laurence. <u>Sound and Sense</u>: An <u>Introduction to Poetry</u>. New York: Harcourt, Brace & World, 1963.

——————————. <u>Story and Structure</u>. 2nd ed. New York: Harcourt, Brace & World, 1966.

An alternative is that of extending the line of dashes as long or as short as the author's name.

2. A chapter or a part of a book, placed before the title, within quotation marks or underlined, followed by a period (the word "In" may occasionally follow this period to separate two underlined works):

Warren, Robert Penn. "Blackberry Winter." <u>Reading Modern Short Stories.</u> Ed. Jarvis A. Thurston. Chicago: Scott, Foresman, 1955.

Aristophanes. <u>The Birds</u>. In <u>Five Comedies of Aristophanes</u>. Trans. Benjamin B. Rogers. Garden City, N.Y.: Doubleday, 1955.

This distinction of chapter or part of a book is not usually made in bibliographies except when the work is separately edited, translated, or written. For example, note the following:

Child, Harold. "Jane Austen." <u>The Cambridge History of English Literature</u>. Ed. A. W. Ward and A. R. Waller. London: Cambridge Univ. Press, 1927. XII, 231–44.

Since "Jane Austen" is *not* a separately published work, your bibliography entry may also read:

Ward, A. W., and A. R. Waller, eds. <u>The Cambridge History of English Literature</u>. 15 vols. London: Cambridge Univ. Press, 1927.

3. The title of the work, underlined, followed by a period:

Stock, Noel. <u>The Life of Ezra Pound</u>. New York: Pantheon, 1970.

4. The name of the editor or translator, preceded by "Ed." or "Trans."

Lagercrantz, Olof. <u>From Hell to Paradise</u>: <u>Dante and His Comedy</u>. Trans. Alan Blair. New York: Washington Square Press, 1966.

However, if the work is a collection or if the editor's or translator's work rather than the text is under discussion, place the editor's or translator's name first, followed by a comma, followed by "ed." or "eds." or "trans." without further punctuation:

Craig, Hardin, ed. <u>The Complete Works of Shakespeare</u>. Rev. ed. Chicago: Scott, Foresman, 1961.

Ciardi, John, trans. <u>The Purgatorio</u>, by Dante. New York: New American Library, 1961.

5. Edition used, whenever it is not the first, in Arabic numerals (for example, "2nd ed."), without further punctuation:

Arbuthnot, May Hill. <u>Children and Books</u>. 3rd ed. Chicago: Scott, Foresman, 1964.

6. The name of the series, without quotation marks and not underlined, followed by a comma, followed by the number of this work in the series in Arabic numerals (for example, "vol. 3," "No. 3," or simply "3"), followed by a period:

Fowler, David. <u>Piers the Plowman</u>. Univ. of Washington Publications in Lang. and Lit., 16. Seattle: Univ. of Washington Press, 1961.

7. The number of volumes with this particular title, if more than one, in Arabic numerals (for example, "6 vols."):

Parrington, Vernon L. <u>Main Currents in American Thought</u>. 3 vols. New York: Harcourt, Brace, 1927–32.
Note that the volumes were not published in the same year.

8. The place, publisher, and date of publication, followed by a period (for example, "New York: Macmillan, 1967."). Whenever more than one place of publication appears on the title page, the first city mentioned is usually sufficient. Also, if successive dates of copyright are given, the most recent is usually sufficient (unless your study is specifically concerned with an earlier edition):

Steinbeck, John. <u>The Grapes of Wrath</u>. New York: Viking Press, 1939.

Include full information for a modern reprint:

Weaver, Raymond. "Introduction." <u>The Shorter Novels of Herman Melville</u>. 1928; rpt. New York: Premier-Fawcett, 1960.

Include the name of the state if necessary for clarity:

> Blum, Robert, ed. <u>Cultural</u> <u>Affairs</u> <u>and</u> <u>Foreign</u> <u>Rela-</u>
> <u>tions</u>. The American Assembly Series. Englewood
> Cliffs, N. J.: Prentice-Hall, 1963.

If the place or date of publication is not provided, insert either "n.p." or "n.d.":

> Bouret, Jean. <u>The</u> <u>Life</u> <u>and</u> <u>Work</u> <u>of</u> <u>Toulouse</u> <u>Lautrec</u>.
> Trans. Daphne Woodward. New York: Abrams, n.d.
>
> Lowell, James Russell. <u>Democracy</u>. N.p., 1886.

9. The volume number, in capital Roman numerals, preceded and followed by a comma, only if you find it necessary to specify such information (and the occasions are rare because you will normally insert only the total number of volumes, for example, "5 vols."). Remember that your footnote contains the specific location of the material:

> Child, Harold. "Jane Austen." <u>The</u> <u>Cambridge</u> <u>History</u> <u>of</u>
> <u>English</u> <u>Literature</u>. Ed. A. W. Ward and A. R.
> Waller. London: Cambridge Univ. Press, 1927. XII,
> 231-44.

10. Page numbers of the entire selection, in Arabic numerals, preceded by a comma and followed by a period. Again, supply this information only upon rare occasions (see item 9 above and item 2, p. 119).

Sample Bibliography Entries — Books

Author

> Cosbey, Robert C. <u>The</u> <u>Writer's</u> <u>Job</u>. Glenview, Ill.:
> Scott, Foresman, 1966.

Author, *anonymous*

> <u>The</u> <u>Song</u> <u>of</u> <u>Roland</u>. Trans. Frederick Bliss Luquines.
> New York: Macmillan, 1960.
>
> > Usually, you should alphabetize this entry by the "S" of the first
> > important word of the title, but alphabetizing by the "T" is also a
> > common practice.

Author, *anonymous but name supplied*

> [Madison, James.] <u>All</u> <u>Impressments</u> <u>Unlawful</u> <u>and</u> <u>Inadmis-</u>
> <u>sable</u>. Boston: William Pelham, 1804.

Author, *pseudonymous but name supplied*

> Slender, Robert [Freneau, Philip]. <u>Letters</u> <u>on</u> <u>Various</u>
> <u>and</u> <u>Important</u> <u>Subjects</u>. Philadelphia: D. Hogan,
> 1799.

Author, *more than one work by the same author*

> Perrine, Laurence. <u>Sound</u> <u>and</u> <u>Sense</u>: <u>An</u> <u>Introduction</u> <u>to</u>
> <u>Poetry</u>. New York: Harcourt, Brace & World, 1963.
>
> ———————————. <u>Story</u> <u>and</u> <u>Structure</u>. 2nd ed. New York:
> Harcourt, Brace & World, 1966.
>
> Rather than repeat the author's name in succeeding entries, insert
> 12 continuous typewriter dashes, above the line, or extend a line of
> dashes as long or as short as the author's name.

Authors, *two*

> Brooks, Cleanth, and Robert Penn Warren. <u>Understanding</u>
> <u>Poetry</u>. 3rd ed. New York: Holt, 1960.
>
> Although the first author's name is inverted, the other's is not.

Authors, *three*

> Hein, Fred V., Dana L. Farnsworth, and Charles E.
> Richardson. <u>Living</u>: <u>Health</u>, <u>Behavior</u>, <u>and</u> Environ-
> <u>ment</u>. 5th ed. Glenview, Ill.: Scott, Foresman,
> 1970.

Authors, *more than three*

> Baugh, Albert C., Tucker Brooke, Samuel C. Chew, Kemp
> Malone, and George Sherburn. <u>A</u> <u>Literary</u> <u>History</u> <u>of</u>
> <u>England.</u> 2nd ed. New York: Appleton, 1967.
>
> An alternative to this form is the use of "et al." or "and others," as
> follows:
>
> Baugh, Albert C., et al. <u>A</u> <u>Literary</u> <u>History</u> <u>of</u> <u>England</u>.
> 2nd ed. New York: Appleton, 1967.

Bibles

> The Bible.
>
> The Bible. Revised Standard Version.
>
> The King James Version is assumed unless you specify another
> version.

Classical works

> Homer. <u>The</u> <u>Iliad</u>. Trans. Richard Lattimore. Chicago:
> Univ. of Chicago Press, 1951.
>
> Shorey, Paul, trans. <u>The</u> <u>Republic</u>, by Plato. Cambridge,
> Mass.: Harvard Univ. Press, 1937.
>
> Use the translator's name first if his work rather than the text is under
> discussion (see p. 120).

Component part of a book

> Browning, Robert. "My Last Duchess." <u>Better</u> <u>Reading</u>
> <u>Two</u>: <u>Literature</u>. Ed. Walter Blair, John Gerber,
> and Eugene Garber. 4th ed. Chicago: Scott,
> Foresman, 1966.
>
> See item 2, p. 119.

Corporate authorship

Committee on Telecommunications. <u>Reports</u> <u>on</u> <u>Selected</u>
<u>Topics</u> <u>in</u> <u>Telecommunications</u>. New York: National
Academy of Sciences, National Research Council,
1970.

Edition

Arbuthnot, May Hill. <u>Children</u> <u>and</u> <u>Books</u>. 3rd ed. Chicago: Scott, Foresman, 1964.

Editor

Shackford, James Atkins. <u>David</u> <u>Crockett</u>: <u>The</u> <u>Man</u> <u>and</u>
<u>the</u> <u>Legend</u>. Ed. John B. Shackford. Chapel Hill,
N.C.: Univ. of North Carolina Press, 1956.

Craig, Hardin, ed. <u>The</u> <u>Complete</u> <u>Works</u> <u>of</u> <u>Shakespeare</u>.
Rev. ed. Chicago: Scott, Foresman, 1961.

If the work is a collection or if the editor's work rather than the text
is under discussion, place the editor's name first (see item 4, pp. 119–
20).

Encyclopedia

Chesterton, Gilbert Keith, and Kenneth J. Fielding.
"Dickens." <u>Encyclopaedia</u> <u>Britannica</u>. 1968.

Illustrations

Venturi, Lionello. <u>Botticelli</u>. With 50 Plates. Green-
wich, Conn.: Fawcett, n.d.

<u>Honoré</u> <u>Daumier</u>: <u>Drawings</u> <u>and</u> <u>Watercolors</u>. Selected and
with introduction by Jean Adhémar. With 58 Illus-
trations. New York: Macmillan, 1954.

Introduction

Webb, Walter Prescott. <u>The</u> <u>Great</u> <u>Frontier</u>. Introduction
by Arnold J. Toynbee. Austin, Texas: Univ. of
Texas Press, 1964.

Manuscript collections

British Museum. <u>Cotton</u> <u>Vitellius</u>, A. XV.

Corpus Christi College, Cambridge. MS CCCC 201.

Play, *classical*

Shakespeare, William. <u>Macbeth</u>. In <u>Shakespeare</u>: <u>Twenty-</u>
<u>Three</u> <u>Plays</u> <u>and</u> <u>the</u> <u>Sonnets</u>. Ed. T. M. Parrott.
New York: Scribner's, 1953.

or

Parrott, T. M., ed. <u>Shakespeare</u>: <u>Twenty-Three</u> <u>Plays</u>
<u>and</u> <u>the</u> <u>Sonnets</u>. New York: Scribner's, 1953.

See item 2, p. 119, and item 4, pp. 119–20.

Play, *modern*

> Greene, Graham. The Complaisant Lover. New York:
> Viking Press, 1959.

Poem, *classical*

> Dante. The Divine Comedy. Trans. Lawrence Grant White.
> New York: Pantheon, 1948.

> Ciardi, John, trans. The Purgatorio, by Dante. New
> York: New American Library, 1961.
>
> > Use the translator's name first if his work rather than the text is under
> > discussion (see p. 120).

Poem, *modern*

> Warren, Robert Penn. You, Emperors, and Others: Poems
> 1957–1960. New York: Random House, 1960.

> Keats, John. "Ode to a Nightingale." Beginnings in
> Poetry. Ed. William J. Martz. Chicago: Scott,
> Foresman, 1965.

Reprint

> Weaver, Raymond. "Introduction." The Shorter Novels
> of Herman Melville. 1928; rpt. New York; Premier–
> Fawcett, 1960.

Series, *numbered and unnumbered*

> Fowler, David. Piers the Plowman. Univ. of Washington
> Publications in Lang. and Lit., 16. Seattle:
> Univ. of Washington Press, 1961.

> Gibson, Lawrence Henry. The Coming of the Revolution:
> 1763–1775. Ed. Henry Steele Commager and Richard
> B. Morris. The New American Nation Series. New
> York: Harper, 1954.

Series, *paperback*

> Commager, Henry Steele. The Nature and the Study of
> History. Social Science Seminar Series. Columbus,
> Ohio: Merrill, 1965.

> Wilson, Howard E. "Education, Foreign Policy, and Inter-
> national Relations." Cultural Affairs and Foreign
> Relations. Ed. Robert Blum. The American Assembly
> Series. Englewood Cliffs, N.J.: Prentice–Hall,
> 1963.

> > or

> Blum, Robert, ed. Cultural Affairs and Foreign Rela-
> tions. The American Assembly Series. Englewood
> Cliffs, N.J.: Prentice–Hall, 1963.
>
> > Preferably, use the latter form; see item 2, p. 119, and item 6, p. 120.

Translator

> Lagercrantz, Olof. From Hell to Paradise: Dante and His
> Comedy. Trans. Alan Blair. New York: Washington
> Square Press, 1966.

Ciardi, John, trans. The Purgatorio, by Dante. New York: New American Library, 1961.

If the translator's work rather than the text is under discussion, place the translator's name first (see item 4, pp. 119–20).

Volumes, *a work of several volumes*

Parrington, Vernon L. Main Currents in American Thought. 3 vols. New York: Harcourt, Brace, 1927–32.

Volumes, *one of several volumes*

Perry, Bliss. The American Spirit in Literature. In The Chronicles of America Series. Ed. Allen Johnson. 48 vols. New Haven: Yale Univ. Press, 1918.

It is seldom necessary to include a specific volume number in the bibliography entry (see below).

Volumes, *component part of one of several volumes*

Child, Harold. "Jane Austen." The Cambridge History of English Literature. Ed. A. W. Ward and A. R. Waller. London: Cambridge Univ. Press, 1927. XII, 231–44.

or

Ward, A. W., and A. R. Waller, eds. The Cambridge History of English Literature. 15 vols. London: Cambridge Univ. Press, 1927.

For a discussion of these entries, see p. 119.

Works alphabetically arranged

Dictionary of American Biography. Ed. Allen Johnson and Dumas Malone. 20 vols. New York: Scribner's, 1928–37.

or

Alden, Edmund K. "Alden, John." Dictionary of American Biography. Ed. Allen Johnson and Dumas Malone. New York: Scribner's, 1928–37.

For a discussion of these entries, see p. 107 and item 2, p. 119.

BIBLIOGRAPHY FORM—PERIODICALS

As you recall, the footnote entry for a periodical article employs the following form:

[1]Jesse Bier, "Weberism, Franklin, and the Transcendental Style," New England Quarterly, 43 (June 1970), 180.

The bibliography entry for this same reference differs in only three ways:

1. The author's name is flush with the left margin, without a numeral, and with succeeding lines indented approximately five spaces.

Enter the surname first, followed by a comma, followed by a given name or initials, followed by a period:

```
Bier, Jesse.   "Weberism, Franklin, and the Transcen-
     dental Style."  New England Quarterly,  43 (June
     1970), 179-92.
```

2. Place a period after the title of the article (see example above).

3. Provide page numbers for the entire article, not for specific pages cited (see example above).

Note below an entry written first for the footnote and then for the bibliography:

```
4Dean T. Mace, "Pietro Bembo and the Literary Or-
igins of the Italian Madrigal," Musical Quarterly, 55
(Jan. 1969), 66.

Mace, Dean T. "Pietro Bembo and the Literary Origins of
     the Italian Madrigal." Musical Quarterly, 55 (Jan.
     1969), 65-86.
```

Sample Bibliography Entries — Periodicals

```
Calitri, Charles J.   "Love Affair with Words." Review
     of This Is Reading, by Frank G. Jennings.  Saturday
     Review, 20 Feb. 1965, pp. 88-89.
```

Note that the above is a weekly magazine, thus no parentheses for dates.

```
DeMott, Benjamin.   "Saul Bellow and the Dogmas of Pos-
     sibility."  Saturday Review, 7 Feb. 1970, pp. 25-29,
     37.

Kilchenmann, Ruth.   "Traum und Wirklichkeit in den
     Werken Friedrich Schnacks."  German Quarterly,
     34 (May 1961), 257-63.

Mothersill, Mary.   "Moral Knowledge." Journal of Philos-
     ophy, 56 (10 Sept. 1959), 755-63.
```

Since this journal is published fortnightly, yet is paged continuously through each volume, a more specific date is provided.

```
Phillips, Norma.   "The Sacred Fount:  The Narrator and
     the Vampires."  PMLA, 76, No. 4, Pt. 1 (Sept. 1961),
     407-12.
```

Note the additional data to show an issue, paged separately, that appears in two parts. Also, *PMLA* is the name of the journal, not an abbreviation.

```
Cottrell, Leonard.   "How Egypt Lived and Died."
     Réalités, March 1970, pp. 52-59.
```

Use this form for a monthly periodical that is paged separately.

```
Sommer, Frank H.   "The Iconography of Action:  Bernini's
     Ludovica Albertone."  Art Quarterly,  33 (Spring
     1970), 30-38.

Ogburn, Charlton, Jr.   "The Motorcar vs. America."
     American Heritage, 21, No. 4 (June 1970), 104-10.
```

Adding an issue number may simplify the reader's search for this journal published every other month and paged separately.

BIBLIOGRAPHY FORM—PUBLIC DOCUMENTS

Since the nature of public documents is so varied, the form of the entry cannot be standardized. Therefore, common sense tells you to provide sufficient information so that the reader can easily locate the reference. Note the following:

U.S. Bureau of the Budget. Special Analysis: Budget of the United States. Fiscal year 1967. Washington, D.C.: GPO, 1966.

Higher Education Act of 1965. 79 Stat. (1965).

> Compare *Swain v. Alabama* below. Court cases and legislative acts follow a form stipulated by law publications. The act or case is listed first, followed by the volume number, abbreviated title, the date of the work in which the act or case is found. Also, notice that the volume number is in Arabic numerals, that the date is placed within parentheses, and that a court case is italicized but an act is not.

Swain v. Alabama, 380 U.S. (1965).

Kansas. Session Laws 1963.

> Normally, the date is placed in parentheses, but in this case the date is a part of the title.

U.S. Congress. Senate Joint Resolution 1. 89th Cong., 1st sess., 1965.

U.S. Congressional Record. Vol. CX.

U.S. Constitution. Art. 2, sec. 1.

U.S. Department of State. Foreign Relations of the United States: Diplomatic Papers, 1943. Washington, D.C., 1944.

U.S. Department of State. United States Treaties and Other International Agreements. XV, Part 1, 1964.

U.S. House of Representatives. Committee on Interstate and Foreign Commerce. Federal Cigarette Labeling and Advertising Act. 89th Cong., 1st sess., 1965. H. Rept. 449 to accompany H. R. 3014.

U.S. President. Public Papers of the Presidents of the United States. Washington, D.C.: Office of the Federal Registrar, 1964.

U.S. Senate. Committee on Foreign Relations. Hearings on S. 2793, Supplemental Foreign Assistance Fiscal Year 1966—Vietnam. 89th Cong., 2nd sess., 1966.

U.S. Senate. The Constitution of the United States of America: Analysis and Interpretation. Senate Document 170, 82nd Cong., 2nd sess., 1952.

U.S. Statutes at Large. LXXVIII, 990.

U.S. Statutes at Large. LXXII, Part 1, 455.

BIBLIOGRAPHY FORM—OTHER SOURCES
Bulletin

French, Earl. "Personal Problems in Industrial Research
and Development." Ithaca, N.Y., 1963. (Bulletin
of the New York State School of Industrial and
Labor Relations, No. 51.)

Dissertation, *published*

Nykrog, Per. Les Fabliaux: Etude d'histoire littéraire
et de stylistique médiévale. Diss. Aarhus, 1957.
Copenhagen: Munksgaard, 1957.

Dissertation, *unpublished*

Phillips, Emmett Loy. "A Study of Aesthetic Distance in
Thoreau's Walden." Diss. Univ. of Oklahoma 1970.

Interview

Interview with Bill Rayson, Director, Credit Bureau,
Tulsa, Oklahoma, May 2, 1970.

Lecture

Jones, Charles. "Thomas Jefferson." Emporia, Kansas,
1965. (Lecture presented at Kansas State Teachers
College.)

Letter, *personal*

Information in a letter to the author from William Inge,
playwright, February 4, 1966.

Mimeographed material

Smith, Jane. "Terms for the Study of Fiction." Cleveland, 1970. (Mimeographed.)

Monograph

NEA Research Division. Kindergarten Practices, 1961.
Washington, D.C., 1962. (Monograph 1962-M2.)

Veeder, William R. W.B. Yeats: The Rhetoric of Repetition. Univ. of California English Studies, 34.
Berkeley: Univ. of California Press, 1968.

Newspaper

Peterson, John. "Assault on Heart Disease." National
Observer, 20 July 1970, p. 1, cols. 4-5, and p.
17, cols, 1-6.

Editorial. "The Irregular Intellectuals." National
Observer, 20 July 1970, p. 10.

Pamphlet

> U.S. Civil Service Commission. <u>The Human Equation:</u>
> <u>Working in Personnel for the Federal Government.</u>
> Pamphlet 76. Washington, D.C.: GPO, May 1970.

Public address

> Sarnoff, David. "Television: A Channel for Freedom."
> Detroit, 1961. (Address presented at the
> University of Detroit Academic Convocation.)

Recording

> "Chaucer: The Nun's Priest's Tale." Narrated in Middle
> English by Robert Ross. Caedmon Recording, No.
> E8C40.

> "I Can Hear It Now: Winston Churchill." Ed. Edward R.
> Murrow and Fred W. Friendly. Narrator, Edward R.
> Murrow. Columbia Masterworks Recording, No.
> E9C10.

Report

> Scheer, Robert. "How the United States Got Involved in
> Vietnam." Santa Barbara, Calif., 1965. (Re-
> port to the Center for the Study of Democratic
> Institutions.)

> Panama Canal Company. <u>Annual</u> <u>Report</u>: <u>Fiscal</u> <u>Year</u>
> <u>Ended</u> <u>June</u> <u>30,</u> <u>1968</u>. Panama: Canal Zone Govern-
> ment, 1968.

Source books

> Wasserstrom, William. "Cooper, Freud, and the Origins
> of Culture." <u>The</u> <u>American</u> <u>Imago</u>, 17 (Winter 1960),
> 423–37. Rpt. in Warren S. Walker, ed. <u>Leather-</u>
> <u>stocking</u> <u>and</u> <u>the</u> <u>Critics</u>. Chicago: Scott, Fores-
> man, 1965.

or

> Walker, Warren S., ed. <u>Leatherstocking</u> <u>and</u> <u>the</u> <u>Critics</u>.
> Chicago: Scott, Foresman, 1965.
>
> Use the form of the first entry if your instructor expects a bibli-
> ography entry for each article from which you cite; otherwise, the
> form of the alternate entry is sufficient.

> Unterecker, John, ed. <u>Yeats</u>: <u>A</u> <u>Collection</u> <u>of</u> <u>Critical</u>
> <u>Essays</u>. Twentieth Century Views. Englewood Cliffs,
> N.J.: Prentice-Hall, 1963.

Television or radio program

> "Town Meeting of the World." C.B.S. telecast, March 1,
> 1966: "Nuclear Proliferation." Narrator, Eric
> Sevareid.

Thesis, *published*

>   See "Dissertation, published," p. 128.

Thesis, *unpublished*

>   Simpson, Herman H. "A Study of Shakespeare's Departures
>   from Plutarch in the Characterization of Cleopatra
>   in <u>Antony</u> <u>and</u> <u>Cleopatra</u>." Thesis Oklahoma State
>   Univ. 1961.

Unpublished paper

>   Elkins, William R. "The Dream World and the Dream
>   Vision: Meaning and Structure in Poe's Art."
>   (Unpublished paper.)

VIII

DOCUMENTATION OF SCIENCE PAPERS

You may discover that your science instructor requires a system of documentation quite different from that described in the preceding two chapters. Accordingly, when you write a research paper in the fields of biological science, physical science, mathematics, or psychology, you should consult this chapter, which is intended to supply a brief but adequate description of science-paper documentation. However, you should realize at the start that modifications of style exist from field to field, and agreement does not always exist within a given discipline. Nevertheless, after consultation with your instructor, you should find one of the two systems outlined below satisfactory for your needs.

As a general rule, science papers, excluding those dealing with physics (see p. 137), require no footnotes except content footnotes (see p. 115). Instead, you insert, within your text, reference numbers (1) or reference dates (1967). Then, at the end of your paper, you list, numerically or alphabetically, only those references actually mentioned in your text. You may label the list as "List of References" or "Literature Cited." The title "Bibliography" seldom appears in science papers.

In addition, you should note other characteristics of the reference entries. First, you will usually capitalize only the first word of titles of books and articles (for example, "The biology of the algae"). But some fields (for example, chemistry and physics) omit completely the title of a periodical article. Second, you will usually abbreviate and seldom underline the name of the periodical (for example, "Amer. J. Bot."; see pp. 150–52, 155–56 for listings of science journals and their standard abbreviations). But you should note that the field of psychology, since 1963, spells in full the names of periodicals. Third, you will usually write the volume numbers in Arabic numbers, although placement and form will vary (for example, "vol. 70" or "70").

Name and Year System

When employing the name and year system, you should place within your text, in parentheses or brackets, the year of publication of the authority's book or journal article. Furthermore:

1. Place the entry immediately after the authority's name:

> Smith (1965) ascribes no species-specific
> behavior to man. However, Adams (1967)
> presents data that tend to be contradictory.

2. If your sentence construction does not require the use of the authority's name, insert both the name and date in parentheses:

> Hopkins (1966) found some supporting evidence
> for a portion of the Marr data (Marr and Brown,
> 1957) through point bi-serial correlation
> techniques.

3. For two authors, employ both names: "(Torgerson and Andrews, 1970)." For three authors, name them all in the first entry, as "(Torgerson, Andrews, and Dunlap, 1970)," but thereafter use "(Torgerson et al., 1970)." For four or more authors, employ "Fredericks et al. (1966)" in the first instance.

4. Use small letters (a, b, c) to identify two or more works published in the same year by the same author, for example, "Thompson (1966a)" and "Thompson (1966b)."

5. If necessary, specify additional information; for example, "Thompson (1967, III)," "(Wallace, 1948, 1967)," and "White and Thurston (1967, 211–214)":

> Horton (1966; cf. Thomas, 1962, p. 89) suggests
> an intercorrelation of these testing devices.
> But after multiple-group analysis, Welston (1967,
> p. 211) reached an opposite conclusion.

6. Alphabetize the "List of References" at the end of your paper. List chronologically two or more works by the same author (for example, Fitzgerald's publication of 1964 would precede his 1967 publication).

A sample "List of References"[1] follows:

List of References

Esau, K. 1965. Plant anatomy. John Wiley and
Sons, New York. 735 p.

Klein, R. M., and D. T. Klein. 1970. Research
methods in plant science. Natural History Press, Garden City, New York.
796 p.

Olive, L. S. 1962. The genus Protostelium.
Amer. J. Bot. 49: 297–303.

------. 1964a. Spore discharge mechanism in
basidiomycetes. Science 146: 542–543.

------. 1964b. A new member of the Mycetozoa.
Mycologia 61: 885–896.

Thomson, W. W., and R. DeTournett. 1970.
Studies on the ultrastructure of the
guard cells of Opuntia. Amer. J. Bot.
57: 309–316.

**Fig. 40: Sample
List of References**

The Number System

After completing your "List of References," you should assign a number to each entry. Then, to designate your source of information, you should employ the appropriate number within your text. Furthermore:

1. Place the entry, enclosed within parentheses (or brackets), immediately after the authority's name:

[1]The form of these botany entries conforms to the *American Journal of Botany, The Botanical Review*, and *Style Manual for Biological Journals* (Washington, D.C.: American Institute of Biological Sciences, 1960).

> In particular the recent paper by Hershel,
> Hobbs, and Thomason (1) raises many interesting
> questions related to photosynthesis, some of
> which were answered by Skelton (2), (3).

2. If the sentence construction does not require the use of the authority's name, employ one of the following three methods:

a. Insert both name and number within parentheses:

> Additional observations include alterations in
> carbohydrate metabolism (Evans, 3), changes in
> ascorbic acid incorporation into the cell (Dodd
> and Williams, 11) and adjoining membranes
> (Holt and Zimmer, 7).

b. Insert both name and number within parentheses and enclose the number within brackets (few journals use this method):

> The subject of the cytochrome oxidase system
> in cell metabolism has received a great deal
> of attention (Singleton [4]).

c. Insert the number only, enclosing it within parentheses (or brackets):

> It is known (1) that the <u>DNA</u> concentration of
> a nucleus doubles during interphase.

3. If necessary, add specific data to the entry (for example, "[3, Proposition 8]" or "[6, p. 76]"):

```
┌─────────────────────────────────────────────┐
│                                             │
│  The results of the respiration experiment   │
│                                             │
│  published by Jones (3, p. 412) had been     │
│                                             │
│  predicted earlier by Smith (5).             │
│                                             │
└─────────────────────────────────────────────┘
```

Arrange your references in alphabetical order and number them consecutively through the list of references (in which case the numbers will not appear in consecutive order in your text), *or* forego an alphabetical arrangement and number the references consecutively as they appear in the text, interrupting that order in your text when entering an earlier reference.

A numbered, alphabetized list follows:[1]

```
┌─────────────────────────────────────────────┐
│                                             │
│              Literature Cited                │
│                                             │
│                                             │
│   1.  Griffeth, T., K. P. Hellman, and R. V. │
│       Byerrum.  1960.  Studies on the biogene-│
│       sis of the ring systems of nicotine.  J.│
│       Biol. Chem. 235:  800–804.             │
│                                             │
│   2.  Hodson, P. H., and J. W. Foster.  1966.│
│       Dipicolinic acid synthesis in Penicillium│
│       citreoviride.  J. Bacteriol. 91:  562– │
│       569.                                  │
│                                             │
│   3.  Kaminskas, Edvardas, and B. Magasanik.│
│       1970.  Sequential synthesis of histidine-│
│       degrading enzymes in Bacillus sybtilis.│
│       J. Biol. Chem. 245:  3549–3555.       │
│                                             │
│   4.  Krebs, H. A., and S. M. Lowenstein.  1960.│
│       The tricarboxylic acid cycle, p. 129–203.│
│       In D. M. Greenberg [ed.], Metabolic path-│
│       ways, vol. 1.  Academic Press, Inc., New│
│       York.                                 │
│                                             │
│   5.  Meister, A.  1965.  Biochemistry of the│
│       amino acids, 2nd ed., vol. 2.  Academic│
│       Press, Inc., New York.                │
│                                             │
│   6.  Smith, I. [ed.] 1960.  Chromatographic and│
│       electrophoretic techniques, vol. 1.   │
│       Chromatography.  Interscience Publishers,│
│       Inc., New York.                       │
│                                             │
└─────────────────────────────────────────────┘
```

Fig. 41: Literature Cited

[1]The form of these biology entries conforms to the *Style Manual for Biological Journals* (Washington, D.C.: American Institute of Biological Sciences, 1960). See also "List of References," p. 133.

SAMPLE FORMS OF ENTRIES FOR THE VARIOUS SCIENCE DISCIPLINES

Biology

> See above, "Literature Cited," p. 135.

Botany

> See above, "List of References," p. 133.

Chemistry[1]

(1) G. C. Pimentel, "The Hydrogen Bond," W. H. Freeman Co., San Francisco, Calif., 1960.

(2) J. D. Corbett in "Fused Salts," B. R. Sundheim, Ed., McGraw–Hill Book Co., Inc., New York, 1964, p. 341.

(3) W. H. Baddley, Ph.D. Dissertation, Northwestern University, Evanston, Ill., 1964.

(4) P. J. Lewi and W. W. Braet, $\underline{J}$. $\underline{Chem}$. $\underline{Doc}$., $\underline{10}$, 95–97 (1970).

(5) G. C. Berry and T. G. Fox, $\underline{J}$. $\underline{Am}$. $\underline{Chem}$. $\underline{Soc}$., $\underline{86}$, 3540 (1964).

(6) J. R. Morton, $\underline{Chem}$. $\underline{Rev}$., $\underline{64}$, 452 (1964).

Geology[2]

Donath, F. A., 1963, Strength variation and deformational behavior in anisotropic rock, p. 281–297 in Judd, Wm. R., $\underline{Editor}$, State of stress in the earth's crust: New York, American Elsevier Publishing Co., Inc., 732 p.

Friedlander, G., Kennedy, J. W., and Miller, J. M., 1964, Nuclear and radiochemistry: New York, John Wiley and Sons, 585 p.

Harker, Alfred, 1965, The natural history of igneous rocks: New York, Hafner, 384 p.

Heard, H. C., Turner, F. J., and Weiss, L. E., 1965, Studies of heterogeneous strain in experimentally deformed calcite, marble, and phyllite: Univ. Calif. Pub. Geol. Sci., v. 46, p. 81–152.

Hill, M. L., and Troxel, B. W., 1966, Tectonics of Death Valley region, California: Geol. Soc. America Bull., v. 77, p. 435–438.

Ziegler, Alfred M., 1970, Geosynclinal Development of the British Isles During the Silurian Period: J. Geol., v. 78, p. 445–479.

---

[1] The form of these chemistry entries conforms to the *Journal of American Chemical Society* and the *Journal of Physical Chemistry*.

[2] The form of these geology entries conforms to *The Journal of Geology, Geological Society of America Bulletin*, and *American Journal of Science*.

Mathematics[1]

> 1. R. Artzy, <u>Linear geometry</u>, Addison–Wesley, Reading, Mass., 1965.

> 2. W. M. Frank, <u>A bound on determinants</u>, Proc. Amer. Math. Soc. <u>16</u> (1965), 360–363.

> 3. I. M. Isaacs and D. S. Passman, <u>Groups with representations of bounded degree</u>, Canad. J. Math. <u>16</u> (1964), 299–309.

> 4. ------, <u>Characterization of groups in terms of the degrees of their characters</u>, Pacific J. Math. <u>15</u> (1965), 877–903.

> 5. C. E. Rickart, <u>General theory of Banach algebras</u>, Van Nostrand, Princeton, N.J., 1960.

> 6. O. Solbrig, <u>Evolution and systematics</u>, The Macmillan Co., New York, 1966.

Physics[2]

> [1]F. Riesz and Bela Nagy, <u>Functional Analysis</u> (Frederick Ungar Publishing Company, New York, 1955), Secs. 121 and 123.

> [2]S. Bergia and L. Brown, In <u>Proceedings of the International Conference on Nucleon Structure</u>, edited by R. Hofstadter and L. I. Schiff (Stanford University Press, Stanford, California, 1963), p. 320.

> [3]Oswald H. Blackwood, William C. Kelly, Raymond M. Bell, <u>General Physics</u> (John Wiley and Sons, Inc. New York, 1963), p. 510.

> [4]T. D. Lee, Phys. Rev. <u>139</u>, B1415 (1965).

> [5]K. Gottfried and J. D. Jackson, Nuovo Cimento <u>22</u>, 309 (1964).

> [6]E. T. Jaynes, Am. J. Phys. <u>33</u>, 391 (1965).

Psychology[3]

> Attneave, F. Dimensions of similarity. <u>American Journal of Psychology</u>, 1950, <u>63</u>, 516–556.

> Gaito, John. (Ed.) <u>Macromolecules and behavior</u>. New York: Appleton–Century–Crofts, 1966.

> Harvey, O. J., Hunt, D. E., & Schroder, H. M. <u>Conceptual systems of personality organization</u>. New York: Wiley, 1961.

---

[1]The form of these math entries conforms to the *Proceedings of the American Mathematical Society*.

[2]Rather than placing these physics notes in a "List of References" at the end of your paper, you should place them as footnotes at the bottom of the page on which the citation appears. The form of these entries conforms to *The Physical Review* and *American Journal of Physics*.

[3]The form of these psychology entries conforms generally to *Publication Manual*, rev. ed. (Washington, D.C.: American Psychological Association, 1957).

Herman, Louis M. Information encoding and decision time as variables in human choice behavior. <u>Journal of Experimental Psychology</u>, 1966, <u>71</u> (5), 718–724.

Keniston, Kenneth. <u>The uncommitted</u>: <u>alienated youth in American society</u>. New York: Harcourt, Brace & World, 1966.

Winett, Richard A. Attribution of attitude and behavior change and its relevance to behavior therapy. <u>The Psychological Record</u>, 1970, <u>20</u>, 17–32.

Zoology

See biology, p. 136, and botany, p. 136.

A GLOSSARY OF ADDITIONAL RESEARCH TERMS

Accents Place where necessary in ink, by hand (for example, *cliché*, *précis*). To determine the correct accents for foreign words, consult an appropriate foreign language dictionary.

Acknowledgments Place necessary acknowledgments or explanations in a footnote to your first sentence:

```
    ¹I wish here to express my thanks to Mrs. Horace
A. Humphrey for permission to examine the manuscripts of
her late husband.
```

Usually, there is no need for a preface in a research paper.

Ampersand Avoid using the ampersand symbol "&." Instead, spell out the "and" in the name of a company or organization, unless custom demands it, e.g., "A&P."

Annotated Bibliography Write descriptive notes for each entry.

Appendix Place additional material in an appendix at the end of your paper. It is a logical location for numerous tables and illustrations or other accumulated data.

Apostrophe Add an apostrophe and *s* to form the possessive of one-syllable proper names that end in *s* or another sibilant (for example, "Keats's poem," "Rice's story," "Bates's *The Kinds of Man*"). In words of more than one syllable ending in a sibilant, add the apostrophe only (for example, "Rawlings' novel," "Evans' essay," "Daiches' criticism"), except for names ending in a sibilant and a final *e* (for example, "Lovelace's enduring appeal").

Arabic Numerals Generally, spell out numbers of less than three digits (for example, "four," "sixteen," "345"), but use numerals for *all* numbers in a paragraph that contains both types. Always spell out numbers that begin sentences. Use the small "l," not a capital "I," when typing the numeral "one." Samples of correct usage:

```
A.D. 200 but 200 B.C.
Art. 3
```

```
Col. 5
eighteenth of November or November 18, 1966
Fig. 6
in 1966-67 or from 1966 to 1967, but not from 1966-67
ll. 32-34
March 5, 1935 or 5 March 1935, but not both styles
1960's but sixties
one-fifth but 153½ (for three or more digits)
pp. 121-22
pp. 1151-53 but pp. 1193-1215
Sec. 3
6 per cent
six o'clock or 6:00 p.m.
6.213
twentieth century
```

Asterisks Use Arabic numerals for footnote numbers and asterisks only for footnoting illustrations or tables (see Fig. 47, p. 146).

Bible Use parenthetical documentation for biblical references in your text—that is, place the entry within parentheses immediately after the quotation, for example, "(II Kings xviii.13)." Do not underline titles of books of the Bible. Abbreviations of most books of the Bible follow (but do not abbreviate one-syllable titles, for example, "Mark" or "Acts"):

I and II Chron.	I and II Chronicles	Lev.	Leviticus
Col.	Colossians	Mal.	Malachi
I and II Cor.	I and II Corinthians	Matt.	Matthew
Dan.	Daniel	Mic.	Micah
Deut.	Deuteronomy	Nah.	Nahum
Eccles.	Ecclesiastes	Neh.	Nehemiah
Eph.	Ephesians	Num.	Numbers
Exod.	Exodus	Obad.	Obadiah
Ezek.	Ezekiel	I and II Pet.	I and II Peter
Gal.	Galatians	Phil.	Philippians
Gen.	Genesis	Prov.	Proverbs
Hab.	Habakkuk	Ps.(Pss.)	Psalm(s)
Hag.	Haggai	Rev.	Revelation
Heb.	Hebrews	Rom.	Romans
Hos.	Hosea	I and II Sam.	I and II Samuel
Isa.	Isaiah	Song of Sol.	Song of Solomon
Jas.	James	I and II Thess.	I and II Thessalonians
Jer.	Jeremiah	I and II Tim.	I and II Timothy
Josh.	Joshua	Zech.	Zechariah
Judg.	Judges	Zeph.	Zephaniah
Lam.	Lamentations		

Capitalization Titles of books: capitalize the first word and all principal words, but not articles, prepositions, and conjunctions (for example, *The Last of the Mohicans*).

Titles of magazines and newspapers: as above, except do not treat an initial definite article as part of the title except when the title is entered separately in a list:

"He was referring to the Kansas City Star and. . . ."

¹⁰Editorial, Kansas City Star, March 18, 1966, p. 43D.

Titles of parts of a specific work: capitalize as for books (for example, "Thompson's Appendix II," "Jones's Preface," "Writing the Final Draft").

Abbreviations: capitalize a noun followed by a numeral indicating place in a sequence (for example, "Act II," "Ch. iv," "No. 14," "Vol. III"). Do not capitalize "1.," "n.," "p.," or "sig."

Titles of French, Italian, and Spanish works: capitalize the first word, the proper nouns, but not adjectives derived from proper nouns.

Titles of German works: capitalize the first word, all nouns, and all adjectives derived from names of persons.

Dash Form the dash with two typed hyphens with no space before or after:

```
The professions that require intelligent, analytic minds
--medicine, law, teaching--attract too few young people.
```

See also p. 147 for sample of the dash in documentation.

Dates Follow these examples:

```
14 March or March 14, not the fourteenth of March
14 March 1967 or March 14, 1967, but consistently use
     one style
March 1967 or March, 1967, but consistently use one
     style
1960's or sixties
in 1966-67 or from 1966 to 1967, but not from 1966-67
150 B.C. but A.D. 150
fourteenth century but 14th century in footnotes
```

Definitions For definitions within your text, use single quotation marks without intervening punctuation (for example, "*et alii* 'and others'").

Enumeration of Items Incorporate short items into the text, as follows:

```
College instructors are usually divided into four ranks:
(1) instructors, (2) assistant professors, (3) associate
professors, and (4) full professors.
```

Present longer items in a tabular form, as follows:

```
College instructors are usually divided into four ranks:

   1. Instructors, at the bottom of the scale, are usually
      beginning teachers with little or no experience.
   2. Assistant professors. . . .
```

Etc. *Et cetera* 'and so forth': avoid using in the text by listing at least four items, as follows:

```
Images of color occur frequently in Crane's writing,
especially blue, gold, red, and grey.
```

Foreign Languages Underline foreign words used in an English text:

```
Like his friend Olaf, he is aut Caesar, aut nihil,
either overpowering perfection or ruin and destruction.
```

Do not underline quotations:

> Obviously, he uses it to exploit, in the words of Jean
> Laumon, "une admirable mine de thèmes poétiques."

Do not underline titles of magazine articles:

> [3]Von Thomas O. Brandt, "Brecht und die Bibel,"
> PMLA, 79 (March 1964), 171.

Do not underline places, institutions, proper names, or titles that precede proper names:

> Of course, Racine became extremely fond of Mlle Champ-
> meslé, who interpreted his works at the Hôtel de Bour-
> gogne.

Illustrations and Tables A table is a systematic arrangement of statistical materials, usually in columns. An illustration is any item that is not a table: blueprint, chart, diagram, drawing, graph, photograph, photostat, map, and so on. Note the following samples:

Fig. 42: Illustration

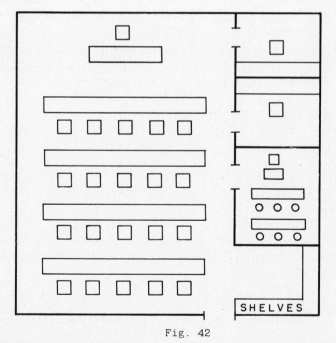

Fig. 42

Audio Laboratory With Private Listening Rooms and a
Small Group Room

Fig. 43: Table

TABLE I

RESPONSE BY CLASS ON VIETNAM POLICY

	Freshmen	Sophomores	Juniors	Seniors
1. Holding action	2	7	19	0
2. Withdrawal	150	137	111	78
3. Escalation	296	301	229	187

When presenting an illustration or table in your research paper, conform to the following stipulations:

1. Present only one kind of information in each illustration, making it as simple and as brief as possible; frills and fancy art work may distract rather than attract the reader.

2. Place small illustrations within your text. Large illustrations should go on a separate page. If you have numerous illustrations or long, complex tables, these should be placed in an appendix at the end of your paper.

3. Place the illustration as near to your textual discussion as possible, although the illustration should not precede your first mention of it.

4. Make certain that your textual discussion adequately explains the significance of the illustration. Follow two rules: (1) write the illustration so that your reader can understand it without reference to your discussion; and (2) write your discussion of the illustration so that your reader may understand your observations without reference to the illustration. But avoid giving too many numbers and figures in your text.

5. In your textual discussion refer to illustrations by number (for example, "Figure 5" or "Table IV, p. 16"), not by a vague reference (for example, "the table above," "the following illustration," or "the chart below").

6. Number illustrations consecutively throughout the paper with Arabic numbers, preceded by "Fig." or "Figure" (for example, "Figure 4"), placed one double space above the caption and centered on the page *below* the illustration.

7. Number tables consecutively throughout the paper with capital Roman numerals, preceded by "Table" (for example, "Table II"), placed one double space above the caption and centered on the page *above* the table.

8. Always insert a caption that explains the illustration, placed *above* the table and *below* the illustration, centered, in full capital letters

or in capitals and lower case, but do not mix forms in the same paper. An alternative is to place the caption on the same line with the number (see Fig. 44 below).

9. Insert a caption or number for each column of a table, centered above the column or, if necessary, inserted diagonally or vertically above it.

10. When inserting an explanatory or reference footnote, place it below both a table and an illustration; then use an asterisk as the identifying superscript, not an Arabic numeral (for example, see Figs. 46 and 47, p. 146).

Note the following samples of charts and illustrations such as you might use in a research paper:

Fig. 44: Illustration

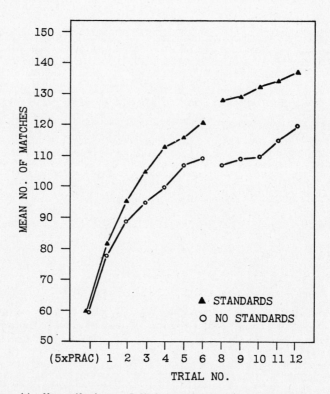

Fig. 44: Mean Number of Matches by Subjects With and Without Standards (By Trial). From Edwin A. Locke and Judith F. Bryan. Cognitive Aspects of Psychomotor Performance. Journal of Applied Psychology, 1966, 50, 289.

Fig. 45: Illustration

SUPRASEGMENTAL

    STRESS /   ∧   \   ∪

    (primary) (secondary) (tertiary) (weak)

    PITCH

     1   2   3   4 (relatively rare)

    (low) (average) (high) (exceptionally high)

    <u>Juncture</u>

      open

      + at minor break, usually between words

      terminal

        | or ⟶ "level"

        at greater break within sentence, also in

          apposition;

              level pitch

        || or ↗ "rising"

        in "yes-no" questions, series;

              pitch-rise before the pause

        # or ↘ "falling"

        at end of most sentences;

              pitch-drop, voice fades off

Fig. 45: Phonemes of English. Generally, this figure follows the Trager–Smith system, used widely in American linguistics. From Anna H. Live, "Pattern in Language," <u>The</u> <u>Journal</u> <u>of</u> <u>General</u> <u>Education</u>, 18 (July 1966), 94.

Fig. 46: Table

TABLE II*

Mean Scores of Six Values Held by College

Students According to Sex

All Students		Men		Women	
Pol.	40.61	Pol.	43.22	Aesth.	43.86
Rel.	40.51	Theor.	43.09	Rel.	43.13
Aesth.	40.29	Econ.	42.05	Soc.	41.62
Theor.	39.80	Rel.	37.88	Pol.	38.00
Econ.	39.45	Soc.	37.05	Econ.	36.85
Soc.	39.34	Aesth.	36.72	Theor.	36.50

*From Carmen J. Finley, Jack M. Thompson, and Albert Cognata, "Stability of the California Short Form Test of Mental Maturity: Grades 3, 5, and 7," California Journal of Educational Research, 17 (Sept. 1966), 165.

Fig. 47: Table

TABLE III.   Inhibitory effects of sugars on the growth of Clostridium histolyticum (11 strains) on nutrient agar*

Sugar added (2%)	Aerobic incubation (hr)		Anaerobic incubation (hr)	
	24	48	24	48
None	11**	11	11	11
Glucose	0	0	11	11
Maltose	0	0	11	11
Lactose	1	1	11	11
Sucrose	3	6	11	11
Arabinose	0	0	0	0
Inositol	0	0	11	11
Xylose	0	0	0	0
Sorbitol	2	7	11	11
Mannitol	9	10	11	11
Rhamnose	0	0	11	11

*From Shoki Nishida and Masaaki Imaizumi. 1966. Toxigenicity of Clostridium histolyticum. J. Bacteriol. 91:481.
**No. of strains which gave rise to colonies in the presence of the sugar.

Parenthetical Documentation Handle references within sentences in one of the following ways:

According to William C. DeVane, A Browning Handbook (New York: Appleton, 1955), p. 37, Browning's liberalism follows the doctrine of Victorian laissez-faire.

or

```
According to William C. DeVane——A Browning Handbook (New
York:  Appleton, 1955), p. 37——Browning's liberalism
follows the doctrine of Victorian laissez-faire.
```

If these forms prove awkward, recast the sentence so that the documentation comes at the end:

```
Browning's laissez-faire liberalism is stressed by
William C. DeVane, A Browning Handbook (New York:
Appleton, 1955), p. 37.
```

Punctuation of Quotations In every instance, place commas and periods *inside* the quotation marks but semicolons and colons *outside* the quotation marks. Place the question mark and the exclamation mark inside the quotation marks if the mark is part of the quoted material; otherwise, place it outside the quotation marks:

```
The philosopher asks, "How should we order our lives?"

How should we order our lives when we face "hostility
from every quarter"?
```

Roman Numerals Use capital or small Roman numerals as shown below:

```
Act II          Bk. x
Vol. III        Chap. xi
Part IV         scene xii
Div. V          canto xiii
Plate VI        pp. xiv-xvii
Table VII
```

A list of Roman numerals:

	UNITS	TENS	HUNDREDS
1	i	x	c
2	ii	xx	cc
3	iii	xxx	ccc
4	iv	xl	cd
5	v	l	d
6	vi	lx	dc
7	vii	lxx	dcc
8	viii	lxxx	dccc
9	ix	xc	cm

Shakespearean Plays For use in parenthetical documentation, the editorial board of the *Shakespeare Quarterly* has approved the following abbreviations of titles of Shakespearean works: *Ado; Ant.; AWW; AYL; Cor.; Cym.; Err.; Ham.; 1H4; 2H4; H5; 1H6; 2H6; 3H6; H8; JC; Jn; LLL; Lr.; Mac.; MM; MND; MV; Oth.; Per.; R2; R3; Rom.; Shr.; TGV; Tim.; Tit.; Tmp.; TN; TNK; Tro.; Wiv.; WT; LC; Luc.; PhT; PP; Son.; Ven.*

Slang Enclose in double quotation marks any words to which you direct attention.

Underlining Underline the following: books, bulletins, pamphlets, periodicals, plays, motion pictures, newspapers, operas, ships, symphonies, and yearbooks. If separately published, underline the following: essays, lectures, poems, proceedings, reports, sermons, and stories.

Word Division When necessary, divide a word with a hyphen so that the break comes between two syllables, but avoid one-letter and two-letter division (for example, "o-ver" or "separate-ly"). When in doubt about the proper division of a word, always consult a dictionary.

APPENDIX II

LIST OF GENERAL REFERENCE BOOKS AND JOURNALS

Applied Sciences

GENERAL

Books

Annual Review of Nuclear Science. Palo Alto, Calif.: Annual Reviews, 1952 – date.

Applied Science and Technology Index. New York: H. W. Wilson, 1958 – date.
> Before 1958, see *Industrial Arts Index.*

Ballentyne, D. W. G., and L. E. Q. Walker. *A Dictionary of Named Effects and Laws in Chemistry, Physics, and Mathematics.* 2nd ed. New York: Macmillan, 1961.

Besserer, C. W., and H. C. Besserer. *Guide to the Space Age.* Englewood Cliffs, N.J.: Prentice-Hall, 1959.

Fleming, Thomas P. *Guide to the Literature of Science.* 2nd ed. New York: Columbia Univ. School of Library Service, 1957.

Fry, Bernard M., and Foster E. Mohrhardt, eds. *A Guide to Information Sources in Space Science and Technology.* New York: Interscience, 1963.

Hawkins, R. R., ed. *Scientific, Medical, and Technical Books Published in the United States of America.* 2nd ed. Washington, D.C.: National Academy of Sciences, 1958.

Hodgman, Charles D., ed. *Handbook of Chemistry and Physics.* Cleveland: Chemical Rubber Publ. Co., 1913 –.

Industrial Arts Index. New York: H. W. Wilson, 1913 – 57.
> Superseded by *Applied Science and Technology Index.*

McGraw-Hill Encyclopedia of Science and Technology. Rev. ed. 15 vols. New York: McGraw-Hill, 1966.

Mellon, M. G. *Chemical Publications: Their Use and Nature.* 4th ed. New York: McGraw-Hill, 1965.

Michels, Walter C., et al. *The International Dictionary of Physics and Electronics.* Princeton, N.J.: Van Nostrand, 1956.

Newman, James R., ed. *The Harper Encyclopedia of Science.* 2nd rev. ed. New York: Harper & Row, 1967.

Pearl, Richard M. *Guide to Geologic Literature.* New York: McGraw-Hill, 1951.

Sternberg, Virgina. *How to Locate Technical Information.* Waterford, Conn.: Prentice-Hall, 1964.

Tannehill, Ivan R. *Weather Around the World.* Princeton, N.J.: Princeton Univ. Press, 1943.

Technical Book Review Index. New York: Special Libraries Association, 1935 – date.

Tower, Merrill E. *A Student Guide for Aeronautics.* Los Angeles: Aero, 1950.

Tweney, C. F., and L. E. C. Hughes, eds. *Chambers's Technical Dictionary.* 3rd ed. New York: Macmillan, 1958.

United Nations Atomic Energy Commission Group. *An International Bibliography on Atomic Energy.* 2 vols. Lake Success, N.Y.: United Nations, 1949 – 51.

U.S. Library of Congress. Science and Technology Division. *Air Force Scientific Research Bibliography, 1950 – 1956.* Ed. G. Vernon Hooker et al. Washington, D.C.: Library of Congress, 1961 –. (In progress.)

CHEMICAL ENGINEERING

Books

Cremer, Herbert W., and Trefor Davies. *Chemical Engineering Practice.* London: Butterworth Scientific Publ., 1956 – 60. (In progress.)

Perry, John H., et al. *Chemical Engineer's Handbook.* 4th ed. New York: McGraw-Hill, 1963.

Journals

Chemical and Engineering News (Chem. & Eng. N.)
Chemical Engineering (Chem. Eng.)
Industrial and Engineering Chemistry (Ind. & Eng. Chem.)
Industrial and Engineering Chemistry Fundamentals (Ind. & Eng. Chem. Fund.)

CHEMISTRY

Books

American Chemical Society. *Chemical Abstracts.* Columbus, Ohio: American Chemical Society, 1907–date.
Clark, George L., et al. *The Encyclopedia of Chemistry.* 2nd ed. New York: Reinhold, 1966.
Crane, Evan Jay, et al. *A Guide to the Literature of Chemistry.* 2nd ed. New York: Wiley, 1957.
Kirk, Raymond E., and D. F. Othmer. *Encyclopedia of Chemical Technology.* 2nd ed. New York: Interscience Encyclopedia, 1963–. (In progress.)
Lange, Norbert A., and Gordon M. Forker, eds. *Handbook of Chemistry.* 10th ed., rev. New York: McGraw-Hill, 1967.
Merck Index of Chemicals and Drugs: An Encyclopedia for Chemists, Pharmacists, Physicians. 7th ed. Rahway, N.J.: Merck, 1960.
Rose, Arthur, and Elizabeth Rose. *The Condensed Chemical Dictionary.* 6th ed. New York: Reinhold, 1961.
Soule, Byron A. *Library Guide for the Chemist.* New York: McGraw-Hill, 1938.
Thorpe, Jocelyn F., and M. A. Whiteley. *Thorpe's Dictionary of Applied Chemistry.* 4th ed. 12 vols. London: Longmans, Green, 1937–56.

Journals

Chemical News (Chem. N.)
Chemical Reviews (Chem. Rev.)
Chemical Society, Proceedings (Chem. Soc. Proc.)
Chemical Titles
Chemistry (Chem.)
Journal of American Chemical Society (J. Am. Chem. Soc.)
Journal of Chemical Documentation (J. Chem. Document.)
Journal of Chemical Education (J. Chem. Educ.)

ELECTRONICS

Books

Carr, Clifford C. *American Electrician's Handbook.* 8th ed. New York: McGraw-Hill, 1961.
Henney, Keith. *The Radio Engineering Handbook.* 5th ed. New York: McGraw-Hill, 1959.
International Dictionary of Physics and Electronics. 2nd ed. Princeton, N.J.: Van Nostrand, 1961.
Knowlton, Archer E., ed. *Standard Handbook for Electrical Engineers.* 9th ed. New York: McGraw-Hill, 1957.
Markus, John. *Electronics and Nucleonics Dictionary.* 3rd ed. New York: McGraw-Hill, 1966.
Sarbacher, Robert I. *Encyclopedic Dictionary of Electronics and Nuclear Engineering.* Englewood Cliffs, N.J.: Prentice-Hall, 1959.
Special Libraries Association. Electrical Engineering Committee. *A Bibliography of Electrical Literature, Current Sources, and Reference Books.* Providence, R.I.: Special Libraries Association, 1928.
Susskind, Charles. *Encyclopedia of Electronics.* New York: Reinhold, 1962.

Journals

Electrical Engineer
Electrical News and Engineering
Electrical Review
Electrical World
Electronic Engineer
Electronic Engineering
Electronic News
Electronics
Electronics Abstracts Journal
Electronics World

ENGINEERING

Books

Dapples, Edward C. *Basic Geology for Science and Engineering.* New York: Wiley, 1959.
Johnson, Irma. *Selected Books and Journals in Science and Engineering.* 2nd ed. Cambridge, Mass.: Technology Press, M.I.T., 1959.
Jones, Franklin D., and Paul B. Schubert. *Engineering Encyclopedia.* 3rd ed. New York: Industrial Press, 1963.
Kent, William. *Mechanical Engineers' Handbook.* 12th ed. 2 vols. New York: Wiley, 1960–61.
O'Rourke, Charles E., ed. *General Engineering Handbook.* 2nd ed. New York: McGraw-Hill, 1940.

Trautwine, John C. *The Civil Engineer's Reference Book.* 21st ed. Ithaca, N. Y.: Trautwine, 1937.

Journals

Engineer
Engineering
Engineering Index
Engineering and Science
Engineering and Science Review
Engineering Designer
Engineering Digest
Engineering Forum
Engineering Journal
Engineering Materials and Design
Engineering News
Engineering Review
International Journal of Engineering Science
Journal of Engineering Education
Professional Engineer (U.S.)

MATHEMATICS

Books

Baer, Reinhold. *Linear Algebra and Projective Geometry.* New York: Academic Press, 1952.

Begle, Edward G. *Introductory Calculus, With Analytic Geometry.* New York: Holt, 1954.

Coxeter, H. S. M. *Non-Euclidean Geometry.* 3rd ed. Toronto: Univ. of Toronto Press, 1957.

Eves, Howard, and C. V. Newsom. *An Introduction to the Foundations and Fundamental Concepts of Mathematics.* New York: Rinehart, 1958.

Feferman, Solomon. *The Number Systems: Foundations of Algebra and Analysis.* Reading, Mass.: Addison-Wesley, 1964.

Feller, William. *An Introduction to Probability Theory and Its Applications.* 2nd ed. New York: Wiley, 1957.

Fletcher, Alan, et al. *An Index of Mathematical Tables.* 2nd ed. 2 vols. Reading, Mass.: Addison-Wesley, 1962.

Guggenheimer, Heinrich W. *Differential Geometry.* New York: McGraw-Hill, 1963.

Halmos, Paul R. *Naive Set Theory.* Princeton, N.J.: Van Nostrand, 1960.

Hurewicz, Witold, and H. Wallman. *Dimension Theory.* Princeton, N.J.: Princeton Univ. Press, 1941.

The International Dictionary of Applied Mathematics. Princeton, N.J.: Van Nostrand, 1960.

James, Glenn, and Robert C. James, eds. *Mathematics Dictionary.* 2nd ed. Princeton, N.J.: Van Nostrand, 1959.

Kelley, John L. *General Topology.* Princeton, N.J.: Van Nostrand, 1955.

Korn, G. A., and T. M. Korn. *Mathematical Handbook for Scientists and Engineers: Definitions, Theorems, and Formulas.* New York: McGraw-Hill, 1961.

Landau, Edmund G. H. *Elementary Number Theory.* Tr. Jacob E. Goodman. New York: Chelsea, 1958.

Lefschetz, Solomon. *Introduction to Topology.* Princeton, N.J.: Princeton Univ. Press, 1949.

Mood, Alexander M., and F. A. Graybill. *Introduction to the Theory of Statistics.* 2nd ed. New York: McGraw-Hill, 1963.

National Council of Teachers of Mathematics Yearbooks. New York: City College, Columbia Univ., 1926 – date.

Parke, Nathan Grier, III. *Guide to the Literature of Mathematics and Physics Including Related Works on Engineering Science.* 2nd ed. New York: Dover, 1958.

Pervin, William J. *Foundations of General Topology.* New York: Academic Press, 1964.

Pontriagin, Lev S. *Foundations of Combinatorial Topology.* Tr. F. Bagemihl, H. Komm, and W. Seidel. Rochester, N.Y.: Graylock Press, 1952.

------------. *Topological Groups.* Tr. Emma Lehmer. Princeton, N.J.: Princeton Univ. Press, 1958.

Suppes, Patrick C. *Axiomatic Set Theory.* Princeton, N.J.: Van Nostrand, 1960.

------------. *Introduction to Logic.* Princeton, N.J.: Van Nostrand, 1957.

The Universal Encyclopedia of Mathematics. New York: Simon and Schuster, 1964.

Journals

ACTA Mathematica (ACTA Math.)
American Journal of Mathematics (Am. J. Math.)
American Mathematical Monthly (Am. Math. Monthly)
American Mathematical Society, Bulletin (Am. Math. Soc. Bul.)
American Mathematical Society, Proceedings (Am. Math. Soc. Proc.)
American Mathematical Society, Transactions (Am. Math. Soc. Trans.)
Annals of Mathematics (Ann. of Math.)
Arithmetic Teacher
Duke Mathematics Journal (Duke Math. J.)
Duodecimal Bulletin (Duodecimal Bul.)
The Fibonacci Quarterly (Fibonacci Q.)
Journal of Algebra (J. Algebra)
Journal of Computer and Systems Sciences (J. Computer & Systems Sci.)

Journal of Mathematics and Physics (J. Math. & Phys.)

Journal of Research of the National Bureau of Standards (J. Res. Nat. Bur. Stand.)

Mathematical Review (Math. Rev.)

Mathematics Magazine (Math. Mag.)

Mathematics Teacher (Math. Teacher)

Philosophia Mathematica (Philos. Math.)

Proceedings of the Royal Society, Series A (Proc. Roy. Soc. Ser. A)

Quarterly Journal of Mathematics (Q. J. Math.)

Recreational Mathematics

Scripta Mathematica

SIAM Review

SRA "New" Mathematics Extension Services

SRA New Mathematics for Today's Teachers (K 6)

Updating Mathematics Services

PHOTOGRAPHY
Books

Abstracts of Photographic Science and Engineering Literature. New York: Columbia Univ. Department of Graphics in cooperation with the Society of Photographic Scientists and Engineers, 1962–date.

Focal Encyclopedia of Photography. Rev. ed. 2 vols. New York: Focal Press, 1965.

1970 Index to Kodak Technical Information. Rochester, N.Y.: Eastman Kodak, 1970.

Photographic Abstracts. London: Scientific and Technical Group of the Royal Photographic Society of Great Britain, 1921–61.

Sowerby, Arthur L. M., ed. *Dictionary of Photography.* 18th ed. New York: Philosophical Library, 1956.

Stubbs, S. G. Blaxland, ed. *Modern Encyclopedia of Photography.* 2 vols. Boston: American Photographic Publ. Co., 1938.

Journals

American Surveyor and Photogrammetrist
Aperture
British Journal of Photography
Image Technology
Industrial Photography
Infinity
Journal of Photographic Science
Leica Photography
Modern Photography
Photographic Society of America (PSA) Journal
Photographic Journal
Photographic Science and Engineering
Popular Photography
Professional Photographer

Technical Photography
Visual

PHYSICS
Books

Condon, Edward U., and Hugh Odishaw. *Handbook of Physics.* New York: McGraw-Hill, 1958.

Glazebrook, Sir Richard T. *A Dictionary of Applied Physics.* 5 vols. New York: Macmillan, 1922–23.

> Largely replaced by *Encyclopaedic Dictionary of Physics*, ed. J. Thewlis (see below).

Gray, Dwight E., et al. *American Institute of Physics Handbook.* 2nd ed. New York: McGraw-Hill, 1963.

Gray, H. J., ed. *Dictionary of Physics.* New York: Longmans, 1958.

Thewlis, J., ed. *Encyclopaedic Dictionary of Physics.* 9 vols. New York: Pergamon Press, 1961–64.

Weld, LeRoy D. *Glossary of Physics.* New York: McGraw-Hill, 1937.

Whitford, Robert H. *Physics Literature.* Washington, D.C.: Scarecrow Press, 1954.

Journals

Advances in Physics (Advances in Phys.)

American Institute of Physics Newsletter (AIP Newsletter)

American Journal of Physics (Am. J. Phys.)

Annals of Physics (Ann. of Phys.)

JETP Letters

Journal of Applied Physics (J. Appl. Phys.)

Journal of Chemical Physics (J. Chem. Phys.)

Physical Review (Phys. Rev.)

Review of Modern Physics (Rev. Mod. Phys.)

Science Abstracts (Section A – Physics)

Art

Books

Adeline, Jules. *The Adeline Art Dictionary.* New York: Ungar, 1966.

American Archives of World Art. *The American Library Compendium and Index of World Art.* New York: American Archives of World Art, 1961.

American Ceramic Society. *Ceramic Abstracts.* Easton, Pa.: American Ceramic Society, 1922–date.

American Federation of Arts. *American Art*

Annual. Washington, D.C.: American Federation of Arts, 1898–1951.
Now called *American Art Directory*.

------------. *American Art Directory.* New York: Bowker, 1952–date.

------------. *Who's Who in American Art.* Washington, D.C.: The American Federation of Arts, 1935–date.

The Art Index. New York: H. W. Wilson, 1929–date.

Boase, T. S. R., ed. *The Oxford History of English Art.* Oxford: Clarendon Press, 1949–. (In progress.)

Canaday, John. *Lives of the Painters.* 4 vols. New York: Norton, 1969.

Chamberlin, Mary W. *Guide to Art Reference Books.* Chicago: American Library Association, 1959.

Champlin, John D., and C. C. Perkins. *Cyclopedia of Painters and Paintings.* 4 vols. New York: Scribner's, 1892.

Chase, George H., and C. R. Post. *A History of Sculpture.* New York: Harper, 1925.

Clapp, Jane. *Art Reproductions.* New York: Scarecrow Press, 1961.

------------. *Museum Publications.* 2 vols. New York: Scarecrow Press, 1962.

Encyclopedia of World Art. 15 vols. New York: McGraw-Hill, 1959–68.

Fielding, Mantle. *Dictionary of American Painters, Sculptors and Engravers.* New York: Struck, 1945.

Gardner, Helen. *Art Through the Ages.* 4th ed. New York: Harcourt, 1959.

Gaunt, William. *Everyman's Dictionary of Pictorial Art.* 2 vols. New York: Dutton, 1962.

Groce, George C., and D. A. Wallace. *New York Historical Society's Dictionary of Artists in America 1564–1860.* New York: Yale Univ. Press, 1957.

Gunnis, Rupert. *Dictionary of British Sculptors 1660–1851.* Cambridge: Harvard Univ. Press, 1953.

Hammond, William A. *A Bibliography of Aesthetics and of the Philosophy of the Fine Arts from 1900 to 1932.* Rev. ed. New York: Longmans, Green, 1934.

Harper's Encyclopedia of Art. 2 vols in 1. New York: Harper, 1937.
Reprinted as *New Standard Encyclopedia of Art* (New York: Garden City Publ. Co., 1939).

Herbert, Robert L., ed. *Modern Artists on Art: Ten Unabridged Essays.* Englewood Cliffs, N.J.: Prentice-Hall, 1965.

The Index of Twentieth Century Artists. 4 vols. New York: College Art Association, 1933–37.

Lake, Carlton, and R. Maillard. *Dictionary of Modern Painting.* 3rd ed. New York: Tudor, 1964.

Maillard, Robert, ed. *Dictionary of Modern Sculpture.* New York: Tudor, 1960.

Mallett, Daniel T. *Mallett's Index of Artists.* New York: Bowker, 1935. Supplement, 1940.

McColvin, Eric R. *Painting: A Guide to the Best Books with Special Reference to the Requirements of Public Libraries.* London: Grafton, 1934.

Monro, Isabel S., and Kate M. Monro. *Index to Reproductions of American Paintings.* New York: H. W. Wilson, 1948. First supplement, 1964.

------------. *Index to Reproductions of European Paintings.* 3 vols. New York: H. W. Wilson, 1956.

Myers, Bernard S. *Encyclopedia of Painting.* New York: Crown, 1955.

New York, Metropolitan Museum of Art. *Library Catalog.* 25 vols. Boston: G. K. Hall, 1960.

Pevsner, Nikolaus, ed. *The Pelican History of Art.* Baltimore: Penguin, 1953–. (In progress.)

Pierson, William Harvey, Jr., and M. Davidson, eds. *Arts of the United States: A Pictorial Survey.* New York: McGraw-Hill, 1960.

The Praeger Picture Encyclopedia of Art. New York: Praeger, 1958.

Read, Sir Herbert E. *A Concise History of Modern Painting.* New York: Praeger, 1959.

------------. *The Meaning of Art.* 2nd ed. London: Faber and Faber, 1936.

Reinach, Salomon. *Apollo.* Tr. F. Simmonds. New York: Scribner's, 1935.

Robb, David M., and J. J. Garrison. *Art in the Western World.* Rev. ed. New York: Harper, 1942.

Smith, Ralph C. *A Biographical Index of American Artists.* Baltimore: Williams & Wilkins, 1930.

Solon, Louis M. E. *Ceramic Literature.* London: C. Griffin, 1910.

Special Libraries Association. Picture Division. *Picture Sources: An Introductory List.* Ed. Helen Faye. New York: Special Libraries Association, 1959.

Sturgis, Russell. *Annotated Bibliography of Fine Art: Painting, Sculpture, Architecture, Arts of Decoration and Illustration.* Boston: American Library Association, 1897.

United Nations Education, Scientific and Cultural Organization. *Catalogue of Colour Reproductions of Paintings Prior to 1860.* New rev. ed. Paris: UNESCO, 1955.

------------. *Catalogue of Colour Reproductions of Paintings 1860–1963.* 2 vols. Paris: UNESCO, 1963.

Vance, Lucile E. *Illustration Index.* New York: Scarecrow Press, 1957.

Who's Who in Art. London: Art Trade Press, 1927–date.

Who's Who in Graphic Art. Ed. Walter Amstutz. Zurich: Amstutz & Herdeg, 1962.

The Year's Art. London: Macmillan, 1880–date.

Journals

American Artist
Art Bulletin
Art Education
Art in Action
Art in America
Art Index
Art Journal
Art News
Artforum
Arts
Arts and Activities
Arts Yearbook
Connoisseur
Craft Horizons
Design
Design Quarterly
Eastern
Everyday Art
Handweaver & Craftsman
International Studio
Journal of Aesthetics and Art Criticism
Liturgical Arts
Magazine of Art
Motif
Portfolio
School Arts Book
School Arts Magazine
Studies in Art Education

Biological Sciences

Books

Agricultural Index. New York: H. W. Wilson, 1919–64.

> Now titled *Biological and Agricultural Index.*

Altman, Philip L., and D. S. Sittmer, eds. *Biology Data Book.* Washington, D.C.: Federation of American Societies for Experimental Biology, 1964.

The American Yearbook: A Record of Events and Progress. New York: Appleton, 1911–51.

Annotated Bibliography of Economic Geology. Lancaster, Pa.: Economic Geology Publ. Co., 1929–66.

Biological Abstracts. Philadelphia: Biological Abstracts, 1926–date.

Biological and Agricultural Index. New York: H. W. Wilson, 1964–date.

Blake, Sidney F. *Geographical Guide to Floras of the World: An Annotated List With Special Reference to Useful Plants and Common Plant Names.* Washington, D.C.: GPO, 1942–61.

Blanchard, Joy Richard, and Harald Ostvold. *Literature of Agricultural Research.* Berkeley, Calif.: Univ. of California Press, 1958.

California Academy of Sciences. *A Century of Progress in the Natural Sciences, 1853–1953.* San Francisco: California Academy of Sciences, 1955.

Cattell, Jacques. *American Men of Science: A Biographical Directory.* 10th ed. 5 vols. Tempe, Ariz.: Jacques Cattell Press, Arizona State Univ., 1960–62.

Comstock, Anna B. *Handbook of Nature-Study.* 24th ed. Ithaca, N.Y.: Comstock, 1939.

Fernald, M. L. *Gray's Manual of Botany.* 8th ed. New York: American Book, 1950.

Gray, Henry. *Anatomy of the Human Body.* 27th ed. Rev. C. M. Goss. Philadelphia: Lea & Febiger, 1959.

Gray, Peter, ed. *The Encyclopedia of the Biological Sciences.* New York: Reinhold, 1961.

Henderson, Isabella F., and W. D. Henderson. *A Dictionary of Biological Terms.* Ed. J. K. Kenneth. 8th ed. Princeton, N.J.: Van Nostrand, 1963.

Howard, A. V., ed. *Chambers's Dictionary of Scientists.* New York: Dutton, 1951.

Jacobs, Morris B., et al. *Dictionary of Microbiology.* Princeton, N.J.: Van Nostrand, 1957.

Jenkins, Frances B. *Science Reference Sources.* 4th ed. Champaign, Ill.: Illini Union Bookstore, 1965.

Palmer, Ephraim L. *Fieldbook of Natural History.* New York: Whittlesey House, 1949.

Sarton, George. *Introduction to the History of Science.* 3 vols. in 4. Baltimore: Williams & Wilkins, 1927–48.

Smith, R. C. *Guide to the Literature of the Zoological Sciences.* 6th ed. Minneapolis: Burgess, 1962.

Spector, William S. *Handbook of Biological Data.* Philadelphia: Saunders, 1956.

Stedman, T. L. *Stedman's Medical Dictionary.* 18th ed. Baltimore: Williams & Wilkins, 1953.

Thompson, Arthur Landsborouth. *A New Dictionary of Birds.* New York: McGraw-Hill, 1964.

Van Nostrand's Scientific Encyclopedia. 3rd ed. Princeton, N.J.: Van Nostrand, 1958.

Walker, Ernest Pillsbury. *Mammals of the World.* 3 vols. Baltimore: Johns Hopkins Press, 1964.

Willis, J. C. *A Dictionary of the Flowering Plants and Ferns.* 6th ed. Cambridge: The University Press, 1931.

World Medical Association. *Seventy-Five Years of Medical Progress, 1878–1953.* Philadelphia: Lea & Febiger, 1954.

Journals

Advancement of Science
Advances in Botanical Research (Advances Botan. Res.)
Advancing Frontiers of Plant Sciences
American Journal of Anatomy (Am. J. Anat.)
American Journal of Botany (Am. J. Botany)
American Journal of Physiology (Am. J. Physiol.)
American Scientist (Am. Scientist)
Animal Behavior
Annales de l'Institut Pasteur
Annals and Magazine of Natural History (Ann. & Mag. Nat. Hist.)
Annals of Botany (Ann. Botany)
Annals of the Missouri Botanical Garden (Ann. Mo. Botan. Garden)
Applied Microbiology (Appl. Microbiol.)
Archiv für Hydrobiologie
Archives of Biochemistry and Biophysics (Arch. Biochem. & Biophys.)
Audubon Field Notes
Audubon Magazine
Bacteriological Reviews (Bacteriol. Rev.)
Biochemical and Biophysical Research Commission (Biochem. & Biophys. Research Comm.)
Biochemistry (Biochem.)
Biochemistry Journal (Biochem. J.)
Biochimica et Biophysica Acta
Bioscience
Botanical Review (Botan. Rev.)
Bulletin of Aquatic Biology (Bull. Aquatic Biol.)
Bulletin of Experimental Biology and Medicine (Bull. Exptl. Biol. & Med.)
Bulletin of the Atomic Scientists (Bull. Atomic Scientists)
Canadian Journal of Botany (Canadian J. Botany)

Canadian Journal of Microbiology (Canadian J. Microbiol.)
Current Contents
DOKLADY – Biochemistry section
DOKLADY – Biological Sciences section
DOKLADY – Botanical Sciences section
Ecology
Evolution
Experimental Cell Research (Exptl. Cell Research)
Federation Proceedings (Federation Proc.)
General Science Quarterly (Gen. Sci. Quart.)
Genetics
Geological Society of America – Bulletin (Geol. Soc. Am. Bull.)
Geophysical Abstracts (Geophys. Abstr.)
Heredity
Herpetologica
Human Genetics
Hydrobiologica
International Abstracts of Biological Sciences (Intern. Abstr. Biol. Sci.)
International Bureau for Plant Taxonomy (Intern. Bur. Plant. Taxonomy)
Journal of Animal Behavior (J. Animal Behavior)
Journal of Animal Ecology (J. Animal Ecology)
Journal of Bacteriology (J. Bacteriol.)
Journal of Biological Chemistry (J. Biol. Chem.)
Journal of Cellular and Comparative Physiology (J. Cellular & Comp. Physiol.)
Journal of Clinical Investigation (J. Clin. Invest.)
Journal of Ecology (J. Ecol.)
Journal of Experimental Biology (J. Exptl. Biol.)
Journal of Experimental Medicine (J. Exptl. Med.)
Journal of Experimental Zoology (J. Exptl. Zool.)
Journal of General Microbiology (J. Gen. Microbiol.)
Journal of Geology (J. Geol.)
Journal of Immunology (J. Immunol.)
Journal of Lipid Research (J. Lipid Research)
Journal of Mammology (J. Mammol.)
Journal of Molecular Biology (J. Molecular Biol.)
Journal of Paleontology (J. Paleontol.)
Journal of Physiology (J. Physiol.)
Journal of Protozoology (J. Protozool.)
Journal of Wildlife Management (J. Wildl. Mgmt.)
Linnean Society of London Journal (Linnean Soc. London J.)

Mutation Research
National Academy of Sciences—Proceedings (Proc. Nat. Acad. Sci.)
National Wildlife (Nat. Wildl.)
Naturalist
Nature
New York Academy of Sciences, Annals of (Ann. NY Acad. Sci.)
Palaeobotanist
Philosophy of Science
Physiological Reviews (Physiol. Rev.)
Physiological Zoology (Physiol. Zool.)
Plant Physiology (Plant Physiol.)
Plant World
Proceedings of the National Academy of Science (Proc. Nat. Acad. Sci.)
Radiation Research (Radiation Res.)
Review of Applied Mycology (Rev. Appl. Mycology)
Science
Science Education (Sci. Ed.)
Scientific American (Sci. Am.)
Scientific American Monthly (Sci. Am. Monthly)
Scientific Monthly (Sci. Monthly)
Soil Conservation (Soil Conserv.)
Stain Technology
Zeitschrift für Zellforschung und mickroskopische Anatomie

Business

Books

Accountants' Index. New York: American Institute of Accountants, 1921–date.
Brown, Stanley M., ed. *Business Executive's Handbook.* Rev. Lillian Doris. 4th ed. New York: Prentice-Hall, 1953.
Business Periodicals Index. New York: H. W. Wilson, 1958–date.

> For material 1913–57, see *Industrial Arts Index* or *Public Affairs Information Service Bulletin.*

Clark, Donald T., and Bert A. Gottfried. *A Dictionary of Business and Finance.* New York: Crowell, 1957.
Coman, Edwin T., Jr. *Sources of Business Information.* Rev. ed. Berkeley, Calif.: Univ. of California Press, 1964.
Georgi, Charlotte. *Literature of Executive Management: Selected Books and Reference Sources for the International Businessman.* New York: Special Libraries Association, 1963.
Harvard University Graduate School of Business Administration. *A Classification of Business Literature.* Rev. ed. Hamden, Conn.: Shoe String Press, 1961.

Heyer, Carl, ed. *The Encyclopedia of Management.* New York: Reinhold, 1963.
Horton, Byrne J., et al. *Dictionary of Modern Economics.* Washington, D. C.: Public Affairs Press, 1948.
Lazarus, Harold. *American Business Dictionary.* New York: Philosophical Library, 1957.
Munn, G. G., ed. *Encyclopedia of Banking and Finance.* Rev. Ferdinand L. Garcia. 6th ed. Boston: Bankers Publ. Co., 1962.
Nemmers, Erwin E., and C. C. Janzen, eds. *Dictionary of Economics and Business.* Paterson, N.J.: Littlefield, Adams, 1959.
Williams, Robert I., and Lillian Doris, eds. *Encyclopedia of Accounting Systems.* 5 vols. Englewood Cliffs, N.J.: Prentice-Hall, 1956–57.
Winser, Marian (Manley). *Business Information: How to Find and Use It.* New York: Harper, 1955.
Wixon, Rufus, ed. *Accountants' Handbook.* 4th ed. New York: Ronald Press, 1956.

Journals

Accountants' Digest
Accounting Research
Accounting Review
Appraisal Journal
Barron's National Business and Financial Weekly
Better Living
Business Horizons
Business Week
Changing Times
Consumers' Research Bulletin
Dun's Review and Modern Industry
Economic Indicators
Employment Security Review
Factory Management and Maintenance
Federal Reserve Bulletin
Federal Tax Articles
Federal Tax Guide
Financial Executive
Fortune
Harvard Business Review
Human Engineering
Journal of Accountancy
Journal of Finance
Journal of Insurance Information
Journal of Marketing
Journal of Retailing
Kiplinger Washington Letter
Labor Market and Employment Security
Lloyd's Bank Review
Magazine of Wallstreet and Business Analyst
Management Accounting
Management News

Management Review
Monthly Review
Moody's Banks and Finance
Moody's Handbook of Widely Held Common Stocks
Moody's Industrials
Moody's Magazine
Nation's Business
Office Executive
Over-the-Counter Securities Review
Personnel and Guidance Journal
Personnel Psychology
Sales Management
Social Security Bulletin
Standard and Poor's Corporation Records
Supervisory Management
Survey of Current Business
Systems
Tax Executive
Value Line
Wall Street Journal

Education

Books

Burke, Arvid J., and Mary A. Burke. *Documentation in Education*. New York: Teachers College Press, Columbia University, 1967.

Buros, Oscar K., ed. *Sixth Mental Measurements Yearbook*. Highland Park, N.J.: Gryphon Press, 1965.

Clapp, Jane. *College Text Books*. 2 vols. New York: Scarecrow Press, 1960. Supplement, 1965.

Education Abstracts. 16 vols. Fulton, Mo.: Education Clearing House, 1936–date.

The Education Index. New York: H. W. Wilson, 1929–date.

Educational Film Guide. New York: H. W. Wilson, 1936–62.

Educational Media Index. 15 vols. New York: McGraw-Hill, 1964. Supplement, 1965.

Good, Carter V., ed. *Dictionary of Education*. 2nd ed. New York: McGraw-Hill, 1959.

Harris, Chester W., and Marie R. Liba, eds. *Encyclopedia of Educational Research*. 3rd ed. New York: Macmillan, 1960.

International Yearbook of Education. Paris: UNESCO, 1948–.

Monroe, Paul, ed. *A Cyclopedia of Education*. 5 vols. New York: Macmillan, 1911–13.

Monroe, Walter S., and Louis Shores. *Bibliographies and Summaries in Education to July 1935*. New York: H. W. Wilson, 1936.

Public Affairs Information Service Bulletin. New York: Public Affairs Information Service, 1915–date.

Singletary, Otis A., and Jane P. Newman, eds. *American Universities and Colleges*. 10th ed. Washington, D.C.: American Council on Education, 1968.

Textbooks in Print. New York: Bowker, 1926–date.
Formerly called *American Educational Catalog*.

UNESCO. *World Survey of Education*. 4 vols. Paris: UNESCO, 1955–66.

U.S. Office of Education. *Biennial Survey of Education in the United States*. Washington, D.C.: GPO, 1921–62.
Continued by *Digest of Educational Statistics*, 1962–date.

Who's Who in American Education. New York: Who's Who in American Education, 1928–date.

World Year Book of Education. London: Evans. 1932–date.
Sometimes titled *Yearbook of Education*.

Journals

American School Board Journal
Bulletin of the National Association of Secondary School Principals
Childhood Education
Educational Forum
Educational Leadership
Elementary School Journal
Elementary School Teacher
Future Teacher
Harvard Educational Review
Journal of Educational Research
Journal of Experimental Education
Journal of Higher Education
Journal of Secondary Education
Journal of Teacher Education
Junior College Journal
National Elementary Principal
NEA Journal
NEA Research Bulletin
Review of Educational Research
School Executive
School Life
Teachers College Journal

English Language and Literature

Books

Abstracts of English Studies. Boulder, Colo.:

National Council of Teachers of English, 1958–date.

Altick, Richard D., and Andrew Wright. *Selective Bibliography for the Study of English and American Literature*. 2nd ed. New York: Macmillan, 1963.

Arms, George, and Joseph M. Kuntz. *Poetry Explication: A Checklist of Interpretations Since 1925 of British and American Poems Past and Present*. Denver: Swallow, 1962.

Bailey, Richard W., and Dolores M. Burton. *English Stylistics: A Bibliography*. Cambridge, Mass.: The M.I.T. Press, 1968.

Baker, Ernest A. *History of the English Novel*. 10 vols. 1924–39; rpt. New York: Barnes & Noble, 1950.

Baldensperger, Fernand, and Werner P. Friederich. *Bibliography of Comparative Literature*, 3rd ed., 1950; rpt. New York: Russell and Russell, 1960.

Bateson, F. W., ed. *Cambridge Bibliography of English Literature*. 5 vols. New York: Macmillan, 1941–57.

Baugh, Albert C. *A Literary History of England*. New York: Appleton, 1967.

Bell, Inglis F., and Donald Baird. *The English Novel, 1578–1956: A Checklist of Twentieth-Century Criticisms*. Denver: Swallow, 1959.

Bernhardt, William F., ed. *Granger's Index to Poetry*. 5th ed. New York: Columbia Univ. Press, 1962.

Blanck, Jacob. *Bibliography of American Literature*. 4 vols. New Haven: Yale Univ. Press, 1955–63. (In progress.)

Bond, Donald F. *A Reference Guide to English Studies*. Chicago: Univ. of Chicago Press, 1962.

Brenni, Vito J. *American English: A Bibliography*. Philadelphia: Univ. of Pennsylvania Press, 1964.

Bruncken, Herbert, *Subject Index to Poetry*. Chicago: American Library Association, 1940.

Cambridge History of American Literature. 4 vols. New York: Putnam, 1917–21.

Cambridge History of English Literature. 15 vols. New York: Putnam, 1907–33.

Cook, Dorothy E., and Isabel S. Monro. *Short Story Index*. New York: H. W. Wilson, 1953. Supplements, 1956, 1960.

Courthope, William J. *A History of English Poetry*. 6 vols. New York: Macmillan, 1895–1910.

Craigie, Sir William, and James R. Hulbert. *A Dictionary of American English on Historical Principles*. 4 vols. Chicago: Univ. of Chicago Press, 1936–44.

Diehl, Katherine S. *Religions, Mythologies, Folklores: An Annotated Bibliography*. 2nd ed. New York: Scarecrow Press, 1962.

Eastman, Mary Huse. *Index to Fairy Tales, Myths, and Legends*. 2nd ed. Boston: Faxon, 1926. Supplements, 1937, 1952.

Ebisch, Walther, and Levin L. Schücking. *A Shakespeare Bibliography*. Oxford: Clarendon Press, 1931. Supplement, 1937.

English Association. *The Year's Work in English Studies*. London: Murray, 1921–date.

Gerstenberger, Donna, and George Hendrick. *The American Novel 1789–1959: A Checklist of Twentieth-Century Criticism*. Denver: Swallow, 1961.

------------. *Second Directory of Periodicals Publishing Articles in English and American Literature and Language*. Denver: Swallow, 1965.

Gohdes, Clarence. *Bibliographical Guide to the Study of the Literature of the U.S.* 2nd ed. Durham, N.C.: Duke Univ. Press, 1959.

Gray, Louis H., and John A. Macculloch, eds. *Mythology of All Races*. 13 vols. Boston: Archaeological Institute of America, Marshall Jones Co., 1916–32.

Hart, James D. *The Oxford Companion to American Literature*. 4th ed. New York: Oxford Univ. Press, 1965.

Harvey, Sir Paul, comp. and ed. *The Oxford Companion to English Literature*. Rev. by Dorothy Eagle. 4th ed. New York: Oxford Univ. Press, 1967.

Harvey, Sir Paul, and J. E. Heseltine. *The Oxford Companion to French Literature*. Oxford: Clarendon Press, 1959.

Haywood, Charles. *A Bibliography of North American Folklore and Folksong*. 2nd ed. 2 vols. New York: Dover, 1961.

Hornstein, Lillian H., ed. *Reader's Companion to World Literature*. New York: New American Library, 1956.

Jones, Howard Mumford, and Richard M. Ludwig. *Guide to American Literature and Its Backgrounds Since 1890*. 3rd ed. Cambridge, Mass.: Harvard Univ. Press, 1964.

Kearney, E. I., and L. S. Fitzgerald. *The Continental Novel: A Checklist of Criticism in English, 1900–1966*. Metuchen, N.J.: Scarecrow Press, 1968.

Kennedy, Arthur G., and Donald B. Sands. *A Concise Bibliography for Students of English*. 4th ed. Stanford, Calif.: Stanford Univ. Press, 1960.

Kunitz, Stanley J., and Howard Haycraft, eds. *American Authors, 1600–1900*. New York: H. W. Wilson, 1938.

------------. *British Authors Before 1800: A Biographical Dictionary.* New York: H. W. Wilson, 1952.

------------. *British Authors of the Nineteenth Century.* New York: H. W. Wilson, 1936.

------------. *The Junior Book of Authors.* 2nd ed. New York: H. W. Wilson, 1951.

------------. *Twentieth Century Authors: A Biographical Dictionary of Modern Literature.* New York: H. W. Wilson, 1942. First supplement, ed. Stanley J. Kunitz and V. Colby, 1955.

Larousse Encyclopedia of Mythology. New York: Prometheus Press, 1959.

Leary, Lewis. *Articles on American Literature Appearing in Current Periodicals, 1900 – 1950.* Durham, N.C.: Duke Univ. Press, 1954.

Magill, Frank N., ed. *Masterplots.* 6 vols. New York: Salem Press, 1960.

Modern Humanities Research Association. *Annual Bibliography of English Language and Literature, 1920 –.* London: Cambridge Univ. Press, 1921 – date.

Modern Language Association of America. *MLA International Bibliography of Books and Articles on the Modern Languages and Literature, 1921 –.* New York: New York Univ. Press, 1964 – date.

Morgan, Bayard Q. *A Critical Bibliography of German Literature in English Translation, 1481 – 1927.* 2nd ed. New York: Scarecrow Press, 1965.

Moulton, Charles Wells. *Library of Literary Criticism of English and American Authors.* 8 vols. 1901 – 05; rpt. New York: Peter Smith, 1935 – 40.

Northup, Clark S. *A Register of Bibliographies of the English Language and Literature.* New York: Hafner, 1962.

Nyren, Dorothy, ed. *A Library of Literary Criticism: Modern American Literature.* 3rd ed. New York: Ungar, 1964.

Richards, Robert F., ed. *Concise Dictionary of American Literature.* New York: Philosophical Library, 1955.

Sampson, George, ed. *The Concise Cambridge History of English Literature.* Cambridge: Cambridge Univ. Press, 1941.

Sell, Violet, et al. *Subject Index to Poetry for Children and Young People.* Chicago: American Library Association, 1957.

Shipley, Joseph T., ed. *Dictionary of World Literature.* New rev. ed. New York: Philosophical Library, 1953.

Smith, Horatio, ed. *Columbia Dictionary of Modern European Literature.* New York: Columbia Univ. Press, 1947.

Spiller, Robert E., et al. *Literary History of the United States.* 3rd ed. 3 vols. New York: Macmillan, 1964.

Steinberg, S. H., ed. *Cassell's Encyclopedia of World Literature.* 2 vols. New York: Funk & Wagnalls, 1954.

Tate, Allen. *Sixty American Poets, 1896 – 1944.* Rev. ed. Washington, D.C.: U.S. Library of Congress, 1954.

Taylor, Archer, and Bartlett J. Whiting, comps. *A Dictionary of American Proverbs and Proverbial Phrases, 1820 – 80.* Cambridge, Mass.: Belknap Press of Harvard Univ. Press, 1958.

Temple, Ruth, and Martin Tucker, eds. *A Library of Literary Criticism: Modern British Literature.* 3 vols. New York: Ungar, 1966.

------------. *Twentieth Century British Literature: A Reference Guide and Bibliography.* New York: Ungar, 1968.

Thurston, Jarvis, O. B. Emerson, Carl Hartman, and Elizabeth V. Wright. *Short Fiction Criticism: A Checklist of Interpretation Since 1925 of Stories and Novelettes (American, British, Continental) 1800 – 1958.* Denver: Swallow, 1960.

Thompson, Stith. *Motif-Index of Folk Literature: A Classification of Narrative Elements in Folktales, Ballads, Myths, Fables, Mediaeval Romances. . . .* Rev. and enl. ed. 6 vols. Bloomington, Ind.: Indiana Univ. Press, 1955 – 58.

Thrall, William F., and Addison Hibbard, eds. *A Handbook to Literature.* Rev. and enl. by C. Hugh Holman. New York: Odyssey Press, 1960.

Walker, Warren S. *Twentieth-Century Short Story Explication.* Hamden, Conn.: Shoe String Press, 1967.

Wilson, Percy, and Bonamy Dobree. *The Oxford History of English Literature.* London: Oxford Univ. Press, 1945 –. (In progress.)

Woodress, James L. *Dissertations in American Literature, 1891 – 1961.* Durham, N.C.: Duke Univ. Press, 1962.

Journals

Abstracts of English Studies
American Journal of Philology
American Literature
American Notes & Queries
American Quarterly
American Scholar
American Speech
College Composition and Communication
College English
Comparative Literature

ELH (ELH is the title*)*
English Language Notes
English Studies
Explicator
Journal of English and Germanic Philology
Modern Drama
Modern Fiction Studies
Modern Language Abstracts
Modern Language Forum
Modern Language Journal
Modern Language Notes
Modern Language Quarterly
Modern Language Review
Modern Philology
New England Quarterly
Nineteenth Century Fiction
Philological Quarterly
PMLA (PMLA is the title*)*
Renaissance News
Review of English Studies
Romance Philology
Shakespeare Quarterly
Studies in Philology
Victorian Studies

Foreign Languages

GENERAL

Books

Modern Humanities Research Association. *Year's Work in Modern Language Studies, 1929 –*. Cambridge: Oxford Univ. Press, 1931 – date.

Modern Language Association of America. *MLA International Bibliography of Books and Articles on the Modern Languages and Literature, 1921 – date.* New York: New York Univ. Press, 1964 – date.

FRENCH

Books

Bornecque, Pierre, and Jacques-Henry. *La France et sa littérature: Guide complet dans le cadre de la civilisation mondiale.* 2nd ed. 2 vols. in 1. Lyon, France: A.C., ca. 1953 – 57.

Castex, P., and P. Surer. *Manuel des études littéraires françaises.* 6 vols in 2. Paris: Hachette, 1960.

Duby, Georges, and Robert Mandrou. *A History of French Civilization.* Tr. James Blakely Atkinson. New York: Random House, 1964.

Grevisse, Maurice. *Le Bon Usage: Grammaire*

française. 7th ed. Paris: Librairie Orientaliste, 1959.

Lagarde, André, and Laurent Michard. *Collection littéraire: Texts et littératures.* 6 vols. Paris: Bordas, 1961.

Lanson, G., and P. Tuffrau. *Manuel illustré d'histoire de la littérature française.* Paris: Hachette, 1953.

Lévêque, André. *Histoire de la civilisation française.* 3rd ed. New York: Holt, Rinehart and Winston, 1966.

Mansion, J. E. *Heath's Standard French and English Dictionary.* 2nd ed. Boston: Heath, 1939.

------------. *Mansion's Shorter French and English Dictionary.* Boston: Heath, 1950.

Maurois, André. *A History of France.* Tr. H. L. Binsse and Gerard Hopkins. London: Jonathan Cape, 1950.

Miller, Minnie, James R. Nielson, and Jean Leblon. *Précis de civilisation française.* New York: Appleton, 1966.

Nouveau Larousse Classique. 3rd ed. Paris: Larousse, 1957.

Petit Larousse Illustré. Paris: Larousse, 1962.

Journals

French News
French Notes and Queries
French Review
French Studies
Réalités

GERMAN

Books

Allgemeine Deutsche Biographie. 56 vols. Leipzig: Duncker, 1875 – 1910.

Betteridge, Harold T., ed. *New Cassell's German Dictionary.* New York: Funk & Wagnalls, 1958.

Brenner, Emil. *Deutsche Literaturgeschichte.* 15th ed. Wels, Austria: Leitner, 1960.

Brockhaus Konversations-Lexikon. *Der Grosse Brockhaus.* 16th ed. 12 vols. Wiesbaden: Brockhaus, 1952 – 58.

Brockhaus Illustrated German-English, English-German Dictionary. New York: McGraw-Hill, n.d.

Bruhns, Leo. *Deutsche Künstler in Selbstdarstellungen.* Königstein im Taunus: K. R. Langewiesche, 1957.

Bruns, Friedrich, ed. *Die Lese der deutschen Lyrik von Klopstock bis Rilke.* New York: Crofts, 1938.

Der Sprach-Brockhaus. 7th ed. Wiesbaden: Brockhaus, 1956.

Fleissner, O. S., and E. M. Fleissner. *Deutsches Literatur-Lesebuch.* 3rd ed. New York: Appleton, 1959.

Krell, Leo, and Leonhard Fiedler. *Deutsche Literaturgeschichte.* 8th ed. Bamberg: Buchner, 1960.

Lennartz, Franz. *Deutsche Dichter und Schriftsteller unserer Zeit.* Stuttgart: Kröner, 1959.

Loram, Ian C., and Leland R. Phelps, eds. *Aus unserer Zeit: Dichter des zwanzigsten Jahrhunderts.* New York: Norton, 1956.

Martini, Fritz. *Deutsche Literaturgeschichte von den Anfängen bis zur Gegenwart.* 10th ed. Stuttgart: Kröner, 1960.

Mathieu, Gustave, and Guy Stern. *Brieflich Erzählt.* New York: Norton, 1956.

New Wildhagen German Dictionary. Chicago: Follett, 1965.

Richter, Karl. *Deutsche Heldensagen, Neuerzählt.* München: Droemersche Verlagsanstalt, 1957.

Rose, Ernst. *A History of German Literature.* New York: New York Univ. Press, 1960.

Scherer, George A. C. *Selected German Ballads.* Boston: Heath, 1951.

Zucker, A. E. *Amerika und Deutschland: Parallel Lives of Great Americans and Germans.* New York: Appleton, 1953.

Journals

German Documentation Literature
German International
German Life and Letters
German Quarterly
Germanic Review

RUSSIAN

Books

Blinoff, Marthe, ed. and tr. *Life and Thought in Old Russia.* University Park, Penn.: Pennsylvania State Univ. Press, 1961.

Morison, Walter A. *Studies in Russian Forms and Uses.* London: Faber and Faber, 1959.

Müller, V. K. *English-Russian Dictionary.* 6th ed. New York: Dutton, 1959.

Neiswender, Rosemary. *Guide to Russian Reference and Language Aids.* New York: Special Libraries Association, 1962.

Rauch, Georg von. *A History of Soviet Russia.* New York: Praeger, 1957.

Treadgold, Donald W. *Twentieth Century Russia.* 2nd ed. New York: Rand McNally, 1964.

Journals

Russian Language Journal
Russian Review
Slavic Review

SPANISH

Books

Anderson Imbert, Enrique. *Historia de la literatura hispanoamericana.* 2nd ed. 2 vols. Mexico City: Fondo de Cultura Económica, 1961.

------------, and Eugenio Floeit. *Literatura hispanoamericana.* New York: Holt, Rinehart and Winston, 1960.

Augé, C. Y. P., and Miguel de Toro y Gisbert. *Pequeño Larousse Ilustrado.* Paris: Larousse, 1946–47.

Cuyás, Arturo. *Appleton's Revised English-Spanish and Spanish-English Dictionary.* 4th ed. New York: Appleton, 1961.

Eoff, Sherman H. *The Modern Spanish Novel.* New York: New York Univ. Press, 1961.

Flores, Angel, ed. *Historia y antologia del cuento y la novela en Hispanoamerica.* New York: Las Américas, 1959.

Garcia López, José. *Historia de la literatura española.* 7th ed. New York: Las Américas, 1963.

Gonzáles López, Emilio. *Historia de la civilización española.* New York: Las Américas, 1959.

Hamilton Depassier, Carlos. *Historia de la literatura hispanoamericana.* 2 vols. New York: Las Américas, 1960–61.

Hespelt, E. Herman, et al. *An Anthology of Spanish American Literature.* New York: Crofts, 1946.

Northup, George Tyler. *An Introduction to Spanish Literature.* 3rd ed. Chicago: Univ. of Chicago Press, 1960.

Pattison, Walter T., ed. *Representative Spanish Authors.* New York: Oxford Univ. Press, 1942.

Romera-Navarro, Miguel. *Historia de la Literatura Española.* 2nd ed. Boston: Heath, 1949.

Torrente Ballester, Gonzalo. *Literatura española contemporánea, 1898–1936.* Madrid: A. Aguado, 1949.

Velázquez de la Cadena, Mariano, et al. *New Revised Velázquez Spanish and English Dictionary.* New rev. ed. Chicago: Follett, 1967.

Journals

Hispania
Hispanic Review
Visión: Revista Internacional

Health and Physical Education

Books

American Association for Health, Physical Education, and Recreation. Research Section. *Research Methods in Health, Physical Education, Recreation.* Ed. M. Gladys Scott. 2nd ed. Washington, D.C.: American Association for Health, Physical Education, and Recreation, 1959.

Avis, Frederick Compton. *The Sportsman's Glossary.* London: Souvenir Press, 1961.

Belknap, Sara. *Guide to Dance Periodicals, 1931–.* New York: Scarecrow Press, 1950–date.

Bucher, Charles A. *Foundations of Physical Education.* 4th ed. St. Louis: Mosby, 1964.

Bunn, John W. *Scientific Principles of Coaching.* Englewood Cliffs, N.J.: Prentice-Hall, 1965.

Chujoy, Anatole, and P. W. Manchester, comps. and eds. *The Dance Encyclopedia.* Rev. and enl. ed. New York: Simon and Schuster, 1967.

Cooper, John M., and Ruth B. Glassow. *Kinesiology.* St. Louis: Mosby, 1963.

Cummings, Parke. *The Dictionary of Sports.* New York: Barnes, 1949.

Gadan, Francis, and R. Maillard, eds. *Dictionary of Modern Ballet.* New York: Tudor, 1959.

Greenwood, Frances A. *Bibliography of Swimming.* New York: H. W. Wilson, 1940.

Higginson, Alexander Henry. *British and American Sporting Authors, Their Writings and Biographies.* Berryville, Va.: Blue Ridge Press, 1949.

Hoff, Phyllis, Muriel Bower, and Mary Ann Ryder, eds. *Bowling-Fencing-Golf Guide, 1969/1971.* Washington, D.C.: The Division for Girls and Women's Sports, American Association for Health, Physical Education, and Recreation, 1969.

Johnson, W[arren] R[ussell]. *Science and Medicine of Exercise and Sports.* New York: Harper, 1960.

Lovell, Eleanor C., and Ruth M. Hall. *Index to Handicrafts, Modelmaking, and Workshop Projects.* Boston: Faxon, 1936. Supplements, 1943, 1950.

Magriel, Paul David. *A Bibliography of Dancing.* New York: H. W. Wilson, 1936. Fourth supplement, 1941.

Menke, Frank G. *The Encyclopedia of Sports.* 3rd rev. ed. New York: Barnes, 1963.

Minneapolis Public Library, Music Dept. *Index to Folk Dances and Singing Games.* Chicago: American Library Association, 1936. Supplement, 1949.

Moomay, Virginia. *Dance Research.* Washington, D.C.: American Association for Health, Physical Education, and Recreation, 1958.

National Recreation Association. *Guide to Books on Recreation.* New York: Bowker, 1956–date.

Neumeyer, M. H., and E. S. Neumeyer. *Leisure and Recreation.* 3rd ed. New York: Ronald Press, 1958.

Spalding's Official Athletic Almanac. New York: American Sports Publ. Co., 1893–1941.

Van Dalen, Deobold B., et al. *A World History of Physical Education.* Englewood Cliffs, N.J.: Prentice-Hall, 1956.

Weston, Arthur. *The Making of American Physical Education.* New York: Appleton, 1962.

Williams, Jesse Feiring. *The Principles of Physical Education.* 8th ed. Philadelphia: Saunders, 1964.

Journals

American Journal of Public Health and the Nation's Health
American Recreation Journal
American Recreation Society Newsletter
Aquatic Artist
Athletic Journal
Ballroom Dance Magazine
Collegiate Baseball
Dance Magazine
Dance Observer
Dance Perspectives
Dance Scope
Field and Stream
Health Bulletin
Health, Education, and Welfare Indicators
Health, Education and Welfare Trends
Hygeia
Hygiene and Physical Education
Journal of Health and Physical Education
Journal of Health, Physical Education and Recreation
Journal of Hygiene
Journal of School Health
Modern Gymnast
Playground
Public Health Reports
Outdoor Life
Outing
Recreation
Research Quarterly of AAHPER

Scholastic Coach
Sports Illustrated
Today's Health
Track and Field News
World Health
World Tennis

Home Economics

Books

Bitting, Katherine Golden. *Gastromic Bibliography.* San Francisco: priv. pr., 1939.

Dodd, Marguerite. *America's Homemaking Book.* Rev. ed. New York: Scribner's, 1967.

Educational Media Council. *Health, Safety, and Home Economics.* New York: McGraw-Hill, 1957.

Gourley, James E. *Regional American Cookery, 1884–1934: A List of Works on the Subject.* New York: New York Public Library, 1936.

Iowa State College of Agriculture and Mechanic Arts. *Basic Books and Periodicals in Home Economics.* Ames: Iowa State College Library, 1942. Supplement, 1949.

Lincoln, Waldo. *American Cookery Books, 1742–1860.* Rev. and enl. by Eleanor Lowenstein. Worchester, Mass: American Antiquarian Society, 1954.

Mann, George C. *Bibliography on Consumer Education.* New York: Harper, 1939.

Montagné, Prosper. *Larousse Gastronomique: The Encyclopedia of Food, Wine, and Cookery.* Ed. Charlotte Turgeon and Nina Froud. New York: Crown, 1961.

Robertson, Annie I. *Guide to the Literature of Home and Family Life.* Detroit: Gale, 1924.

Simon, André L. *Bibliotheca Gastronomica: A Catalogue of Books and Documents on Gastronomy.* London: Wine and Food Society, 1953.

U. S. Dept. of Agriculture. *Home Economics Research Report.* Washington, D.C.: GPO, 1957–date.

Vicaire, Georges. *Bibliographie Gastronomique.* New York: B. Franklin, 1890.

Journals

Better Homes and Gardens
Changing Times
Consumer Reports
Cookbook Digest
Cuisine et vins de france
Domestic Science
Food and Cookery Review

Good Housekeeping
Home Economics Research Abstracts
Homemaker
Journal of Food Science
Journal of Home Economics
Journal of Marriage and the Family
Journal of Nutrition
Mademoiselle
Vogue
What's New in Home Economics

Music

Books

American Society of Composers, Authors and Publishers. *The ASCAP Biographical Dictionary of Composers, Authors, and Publishers.* 2nd ed. New York: Crowell, 1952.

Apel, Willi. *Harvard Dictionary of Music.* Cambridge, Mass.: Harvard Univ. Press, 1961.

------------, and Ralph T. Daniel. *The Harvard Brief Dictionary of Music.* Cambridge, Mass.: Harvard Univ. Press, 1966.

Baker, Theodore. *Biographical Dictionary of Musicians.* Rev. by Nicolas Slonimsky. 5th ed. New York: Schirmer, 1958.

------------. *Dictionary of Musical Terms.* New York: Schirmer, 1923.

Bessaraboff, Nicholas. *Ancient European Musical Instruments.* Boston: Museum of Fine Arts, by Harvard Univ. Press, 1941.

Chase, Gilbert. *A Guide to the Music of Latin America.* 2nd ed. Washington, D.C.: Library of Congress, 1962.

Clough, Francis F., and G. J. Cuming. *The World's Encyclopaedia of Recorded Music.* 3 vols. London: Gramaphone Corp., 1952. Supplements, 1953, 1957.

A Dictionary of Modern Music and Musicians. London: Dent, 1924.

Duckles, Vincent H. *Music Reference and Research Materials: An Annotated Bibliography.* New York: Free Press of Glencoe, 1964.

Einstein, Alfred. *Music in the Romantic Era.* New York: Norton, 1947.

Ewen, David. *American Composers Today.* New York: H. W. Wilson, 1949.

------------. *Encyclopedia of Concert Music.* New York: Hill & Wang, 1959.

Feather, Leonard. *The New Edition of The Encyclopedia of Jazz.* New York: Horizon Press, 1960.

Grove, Sir George. *Grove's Dictionary of Music and Musicians.* Ed. H. C. Colles. 3rd ed.

5 vols. New York: St. Martin's Press, 1927–28.

————. *Grove's Dictionary of Music and Musicians.* Ed. Eric Blom. 5th ed. 10 vols. New York: St. Martin's Press, 1954–61.

Haydon, Glen. *Introduction to Musicology.* 1941; rpt. Chapel Hill: Univ. of North Carolina Press, 1959.

Hewitt, Helen. *Doctoral Dissertations in Musicology.* 4th ed. Philadelphia: American Musicological Soc., 1965.

Heyer, Anna Harriet. *A Check-List of Publications of Music.* Ann Arbor, Mich.: School of Music, Univ. of Michigan, 1944.

Howard, John Tasker. *The World's Great Operas.* Newly enl. ed. New York: Random House, 1959.

Julian, John. *Dictionary of Hymnology.* Rev. ed., 1925; rpt. New York: Dover, 1957.

Keohn, Ernst C. "The Bibliography of Music." *Musical Quarterly,* 5(1919), 231–54.

King, Alexander Hyatt. "Recent Work in Music Bibliography." *The Library,* 26 (Sept.–Dec. 1945).

Kobbé, Gustav. *Kobbé's Complete Opera Book.* Ed. the Earl of Harewood. New York: Putnam, 1963.

Kolodin, Irving. *New Guide to Recorded Music.* Garden City, N.Y.: Doubleday, 1947.

Láng, Paul Henry. *Music in Western Civilization.* New York: Norton, 1941.

Lawless, Ray M. *Folksingers and Folksongs in America.* New York: Duell, 1960.

Loewenberg, Alfred. *Annals of Opera, 1597–1940.* 2nd ed. 2 vols. Geneva: Societas Bibliographica, 1955.

Martens, Frederick H. *A Thousand and One Nights of Opera.* New York: Appleton, 1926.

McSpadden, J. Walker. *Operas and Musical Comedies.* Enl. ed. New York: Crowell, 1954.

The Music Index. Detroit: Information Service, 1949–date.

Musician's Guide. 3 vols. New York: Music Information Service, 1954–57.

New Oxford History of Music. London: Oxford Univ. Press, 1954–. (In progress.)

Oxford History of Music. 2nd ed. London: Oxford Univ. Press, 1929–. (In progress.)

Pratt, Waldo Selden. *The New Encyclopedia of Music and Musicians.* New ed. New York: Macmillan, 1929.

Reese, Gustave. *Music in Renaissance.* Rev. ed. New York: Norton, 1959.

————. *Music in the Middle Ages.* New York: Norton, 1940.

Reisner, Robert George. *The Literature of Jazz: A Selective Bibliography.* New York: New York Public Library, 1959.

Sachs, Curt. *The History of Musical Instruments.* New York: Norton, 1940.

Scholes, Percy A. *The Oxford Companion to Music.* 9th ed. London: Oxford Univ. Press, 1955.

Shapiro, Nat. *Popular Music: An Annotated Index of American Popular Songs.* New York: Adrian Press, 1964–. (In progress.)

Slonimsky, Nicolas. *Music Since 1900.* 3rd ed. New York: Coleman-Ross, 1949.

Smith, William James. *A Dictionary of Musical Terms in Four Languages.* London: Hutchinson, 1961.

Spaeth, Sigmund. *A History of Popular Music in America.* New York: Random House, 1948.

Strunk, William O. *State and Resources of Musicology in the United States.* Washington, D.C.: American Council of Learned Societies, 1932.

Thompson, Oscar. *The International Cyclopedia of Music and Musicians.* Rev. Robert Sabin. 9th ed. New York: Dodd, Mead, 1964.

————. *Plots of the Operas.* New York: Dodd, Mead, 1940.

U.S. Library of Congress. Division of Music. *Catalogue of Opera Librettos Printed Before 1800.* Ed. O. G. T. Sonneck. 2 vols. Washington, D.C.: GPO, 1914.

Westrup, Jack A., and F. L. Harrison. *The New College Encyclopedia of Music.* New York: Norton, 1960.

The World of Music. 4 vols. New York: Abradale Press, 1963.

Journals

ACTA Musicologia
American Music Teacher
Brass Quarterly
British Catalogue of Music
Clavier
Educational Music Magazine
Journal of Music Theory
Journal of Music Therapy
Journal of Renaissance and Baroque Music
Journal of Research in Music Education
Journal of the American Musicological Society
Modern Music
Music and Letters
Music Journal
Music Journal Biographical Cards
Musica Disciplina
Musical America

Musical Quarterly
Musical Record
Musical Times
Musician
Notes
Opera News
Piano Teacher
Sonorum Speculum

Journal of the History of Ideas
Pacific Philosophy Forum
Personalist
Philosophia Mathematica
Philosophical Review
Philosophy and Phenomenological Research
Self Realization Magazine
Soviet Studies in Philosophy
Studies in Soviet Thought

Philosophy

Books

Baldwin, James Mark. *Dictionary of Philosophy and Psychology*. 3 vols. 1901–05; rpt. Gloucester, Mass.: Peter Smith, 1960.

Bibliography of Philosophy, 1933–1936. 4 vols. New York: Journal of Philosophy, 1934–37.

Hill, Johnson D., and W. E. Stuermann. *Philosophy and the American Heritage*. New York: Philosophical Library, 1961.

Miller, Hugh. *An Historical Introduction to Modern Philosophy*. New York: Macmillan, 1947.

Rand, Benjamin, comp. *Bibliography of Philosophy, Psychology and Cognate Subjects*. 2 vols. New York: Macmillan, 1905.

Runes, Dagobert D., ed. *The Dictionary of Philosophy*. New York: Philosophical Library, 1942.

Russell, Bertrand. *A History of Western Philosophy*. New York: Simon and Schuster, 1945.

Schneider, Herbert W. *A History of American Philosophy*. New York: Columbia Univ. Press, 1963.

U.S. Library of Congress. General Reference and Bibliography Division. *Philosophical Periodicals: An Annotated World List*, by David Baumgardt. Washington, D.C.: U.S. Library of Congress, 1952.

Urmson, J. O., ed. *The Concise Encyclopedia of Western Philosophy and Philosophers*. New York: Hawthorn Books, 1960.

Journals

American Philosophical Society, Proceedings
Bibliography of Philosophy
Ethics
International Journal of Ethics
Journal of Philosophy
Journal of Philosophy, Psychology, and Scientific Method
Journal of Symbolic Logic

Psychology

Books

American Psychological Association. *Psychological Abstracts*. Lancaster, Pa.: American Psychological Association, 1927–date.

Annual Review of Psychology. Palo Alto, Calif.: Annual Reviews, 1950–date.

Buros, Oscar K., ed. *Mental Measurements Yearbook*. Highland Park, N.J.: Gryphon Press, 1938–.

Chandler, Albert R., and E. N. Barnhart. *A Bibliography of Psychological and Experimental Aesthetics, 1864–1937*. Berkeley, Calif.: Univ. of California Press, 1938. (Mimeographed.)

English, Horace B., and Ava C. English. *A Comprehensive Dictionary of Psychological and Psychoanalytical Terms*. New York: Longmans, 1958.

Good, Carter V., and Douglas E. Scates. *Methods of Research: Educational, Psychological, Sociological*. New York: Appleton, 1954.

Gowan, John Curtis, comp. *Annotated Bibliography on Creativity and Giftedness*. Northridge, Calif.: San Fernando Valley State College Foundation, 1965.

Grinstein, Alexander. *The Index of Psychoanalytic Writings*. 5 vols. New York: International Universities Press, 1956–60. Supplements, 1964–. (In progress.)

Harriman, Philip L., ed. *Encyclopedia of Psychology*. New York: Citadel Press, 1946.

Harvard University. *The Harvard List of Books in Psychology*. 3rd ed. Cambridge, Mass.: Harvard Univ. Press, 1964.

Kiell, Norman. *Psychiatry and Psychology in the Visual Arts and Aesthetics: A Bibliography*. Madison: Univ. of Wisconsin Press, 1965.

Louttit, C. M. *Handbook of Psychological Literature*. Bloomington, Ind.: Principia Press, 1932.

Mental Health Book Review Index. New York: American Foundation for Mental Hygiene, 1956–date.

Murchison, C. A., ed. *A Handbook of Social Psychology.* New York: Russell & Russell, 1967.

Psychological Index, 1894–1935. 42 vols. Princeton, N.J.: Psychological Review Co., 1895–1936.
    Superseded by *Psychological Abstracts.*

Journals

American Journal of Psychology
American Journal of Psychotherapy
American Psychologist
Annual Review of Psychology
Behavioral Science
Child Development Abstracts and Bibliography
Contemporary Psychology
Journal of Abnormal & Social Psychology
Journal of Applied Behavioral Science
Journal of Applied Psychology
Journal of Clinical Psychology
Journal of Educational Psychology
Journal of Experimental Psychology
Journal of General Psychology
Journal of Individual Psychology
Journal of Psychology
Journal of Social Psychology
Menninger Quarterly
Psychological Bulletin
Psychological Monographs
Psychological Record
Psychological Review

Religion

Books

American Theological Library Association. *Index to Religious Periodical Literature: An Author and Subject Index to Periodical Literature, Including an Author Index to Book Reviews.* Chicago: American Theological Library Association, 1949–date.

Attwater, Donald, ed. *A Catholic Dictionary.* 3rd ed. New York: Macmillan, 1958.

Barrow, John Graves. *A Bibliography of Bibliographies in Religion.* Ann Arbor, Mich.: Edwards, 1955.

Butler, Alban. *Lives of the Saints.* Ed. Herbert Thurston and Donald Attwater. Complete ed. 4 vols. New York: Kenedy, 1956.

Buttrick, George A., et al. *The Interpreter's Bible.* 12 vols. New York: Abingdon-Cokesbury, 1951–57.

————, ed. *The Interpreter's Dictionary of the Bible.* 4 vols. New York: Abingdon Press, 1962.

Case, Shirley J., ed. *A Bibliographical Guide to the History of Christianity.* Chicago: Univ. of Chicago Press, 1931.

The Catholic Encyclopedia. 18 vols. New York: Gilmary Society, 1950–59.

The Catholic Periodical Index: A Cumulative Author and Subject Index to a Selected List of Catholic Periodicals. New York: Catholic Library Association, 1939–date.

Coulson, John, ed. *The Saints: A Concise Biographical Dictionary.* New York: Hawthorn, 1958.

Cross, F. L., ed. *The Oxford Dictionary of the Christian Church.* London: Oxford Univ. Press, 1957.

Crow, Paul A., Jr. *The Ecumenical Movement in Bibliographical Outline.* New York: Dept. of Faith and Order, National Council of the Churches of Christ in the U.S.A., 1965.

Ferm, Vergilius T. A., ed. *An Encyclopedia of Religion.* New York: Philosophical Library, 1945.

Frazer, Sir James George. *The New Golden Bough.* Ed. Theodor H. Gastner. New York: Criterion, 1959.

Gibb, H. A. R., and J. H. Kramers, eds. *Shorter Encyclopedia of Islam.* Ithaca, N.Y.: Cornell Univ. Press, 1956.

Hastings, James, ed. *Dictionary of the Bible.* Rev. F. C. Grant and H. H. Rowley. New York: Scribner's, 1963.

————, ed. *Encyclopaedia of Religion and Ethics.* 2nd ed. 12 vols. New York: Scribner's, 1908–27.

Illustrated World of the Bible Library. Ed. Benjamin Mazar, Michael Avi-Yonah et al. New York: McGraw-Hill, 1961.

International Association for the Study of History of Religions. *International Bibliography of the History of Religions, 1952–.* Leiden, Netherlands: E. J. Brill, 1952–date.

Joy, Charles R., comp. *Harper's Topical Concordance.* Rev. ed. New York: Harper, 1962.

Loetscher, Lefferts A., ed. *Twentiety-Century Encyclopedia of Religious Knowledge.* Grand Rapids, Mich.: Baker Book House, 1955.
    Supplements *New Schaff-Herzog Encyclopedia of Religious Knowledge.*

Mayer, Frederick E., ed. *The Religious Bodies of America.* 2nd ed. St. Louis: Concordia, 1956.

Mead, Frank Spencer. *Handbook of Denomi-*

nations in the United States. 2nd ed. New York: Abingdon Press, 1961.

Meissner, William W. *Annotated Bibliography in Religion and Psychology.* New York: Academy of Religion and Mental Health, 1961.

Miller, Madeleine S., and J. Lane Miller. *Harper's Bible Dictionary.* New York: Harper, 1952.

Morris, Raymond P. *A Theological Book List.* Naperville, Ill.: Allenson, 1960.

Nelson's Complete Concordance of the Revised Standard Version of the Bible. Comp. John W. Ellison. New York: Nelson, 1957.

Oxford Bible Atlas. Ed. Herbert G. May, R. W. Hamilton, and G. N. S. Hunt. London: Oxford Univ. Press, 1962.

Roth, Cecil, ed. *The Standard Jewish Encyclopedia.* New rev. ed. Garden City, N.Y.: Doubleday, 1962.

Schaff, Philip. *The New Schaff-Herzog Encyclopedia of Religious Knowledge.* Ed. Samuel Jackson et al. 12 vols. 1908–12; rpt. Grand Rapids, Mich.: Baker Book House, 1949–50.

Smith, James Ward, and A. Leland Jamison, eds. *Religion in American Life.* Princeton, N.J.: Princeton Univ. Press, 1961–. (In progress.)

Strong, James. *The Exhaustive Concordance of the Bible.* 1894; rpt. New York: Abingdon, 1963.

Thompson, Newton W., and Raymond Stock. *Complete Concordance to the Bible* (Douay Version). St. Louis: Herder, 1945.

Union Theological Seminary. *Essential Books for a Pastor's Study.* Richmond, Va.: Union Theological Seminary, 1960.

Universal Jewish Encyclopedia: An Authoritative and Popular Presentation of Jews and Judaism Since the Earliest Times. 10 vols. New York: Universal Jewish Encyclopedia, 1939–44.

Wright, George E., and Floyd V. Filson, eds. *The Westminster Historical Atlas to the Bible.* Rev. ed. Philadelphia: Westminster Press, 1956.

Yearbook of American Churches. New York: National Council of the Churches of Christ in America, 1916–date.

Zaehner, Robert C., ed. *The Concise Encyclopedia of Living Faiths.* New York: Hawthorn, 1959.

Journals

America
American Judaism
The Biblical Archaeologist

Catholic Digest
Christian Century
Christian Herald
Christian Scholar
Christianity and Crisis
Church History
Commentary
Commonweal
Cross Currents
Dialog
Ecumenical Review
Ecumenist
Encounter
The Expository Times
Hibbert Journal
History of Religions
International Journal of Religious Education
International Review of Missions
Interpretation: A Journal of Bible and Theology
Journal for the Scientific Study of Religion
Journal of Religion
Motive
Religion in Life
Religious and Theological Abstracts
Religious Education
Risk

Social Sciences

GENERAL

Books

Basler, Roy P., et al., eds. *A Guide to the Study of the United States of America.* Washington, D.C.: U.S. Library of Congress, 1960.

Bellamy, Raymond F. *A Preface to the Social Sciences.* New York: McGraw-Hill, 1956.

Boyd, Anne M. and R. E. Rips. *United States Government Publications.* 3rd ed. New York: H. W. Wilson, 1949.

Chambers's Encyclopedia World Survey. London: G. Newnes, 1952–date.

Clarke, Jack A., ed. *Research Materials in the Social Sciences.* Madison, Wisc.: Univ. of Wisconsin Press, 1959.

Cohen, Benjamin A., ed. *The Worldmark Encyclopedia of the Nations.* 5 vols. New York: Worldmark Press, Harper, 1963.

Commager, Henry S., and Richard B. Morris, eds. *The New American Nation Series.* New York: Harper, 1954–. (In progress.)

Gould, Julius, and W. L. Kolb. *A Dictionary of the Social Sciences.* New York: Free Press of Glencoe, 1964.

Hoselitz, Berthold F., ed. *A Reader's Guide to the Social Sciences.* Glencoe, Ill.: Free Press, 1960.

Lewis, Peter R. *Literature of the Social Sciences.* London: Library Association, 1960.

London Bibliography of the Social Sciences. London: London School of Economics, 1931 –.

New York State Library. *Checklist of Books and Pamphlets in the Social Sciences.* Albany: New York State Library, 1956 – date.

Schmeckebier, Laurence F., and Roy B. Eastin. *Government Publications and Their Use.* Rev. ed. Washington, D.C.: Brookings Institution, 1961.

Seligman, Edwin R. A., and Alvin Johnson. *Encyclopaedia of the Social Sciences.* 15 vols. New York: Macmillan, 1937.

Tompkins, Dorothy C. *Methodology of Social Science Research: A Bibliography.* Berkeley, Calif.: Univ. of California Press, 1936.

United Nations Statistical Yearbook, New York: Publishing Service, United Nations, 1948 – date.

U.S. Library of Congress. Exchange and Gift Division. *Monthly Checklist of State Publications.* Washington, D.C.: GPO, 1912 – date.

U.S. Superintendent of Documents. *Monthly Catalog of United States Government Publications.* Washington, D.C.: GPO, 1895 – date.

White, Carl M., et al. *Sources of Information in the Social Sciences: A Guide to the Literature.* Totowa, N.J.: Bedminster Press, 1964.

Zadrozny, John T., ed. *Dictionary of Social Science.* Washington, D.C.: Public Affairs Press, 1959.

ECONOMICS
Books

American Economic Association. *Index to Economic Journals.* Homewood, Ill.: Irwin, 1961 –62.

Batson, Harold Edward, comp. *A Select Bibliography of Modern Economic Theory, 1870 – 1929.* London: Routledge, 1930.

Commodity Year Book. New York: Commodity Research Bureau, 1939 – date.

Dorfman, Joseph. *The Economic Mind in American Civilization.* 5 vols. New York: Viking Press, 1946 – 59.

Economic Almanac. New York: National Industrial Conference Board, 1949 – date.

Horton, Byrne, ed. *Dictionary of Labor Economics.* Washington, D.C.: Public Affairs Press, 1948.

––––––––––. *Dictionary of Modern Economics.*

Washington, D.C.: Public Affairs Press, 1948.

International Bibliography of Economics. Chicago: Aldine, 1955 – date.

The McGraw-Hill Dictionary of Modern Economics: A Handbook of Terms and Organizations. New York: McGraw-Hill, 1965.

Palgrave, Sir Robert Harry Inglis. *Palgrave's Dictionary of Political Economy.* Ed. Henry Higgs. 3 vols. London: Macmillan, 1925 – 26.

Public Affairs Information Service Bulletin. New York: Public Affairs Information Service, 1920 – date.

Sloan, Harold S., and Arnold J. Zurcher, eds. *A Dictionary of Economics.* 4th rev. ed. New York: Barnes & Noble, 1961.

United Nations. Bureau of General Economic Research and Policies. *World Economic Survey.* New York: United Nations Dept. of Economic and Social Affairs, 1945 – 47 – date.

U.S. Bureau of Foreign and Domestic Commerce. *Foreign Commerce Yearbook.* 10 vols. Washington, D.C.: GPO, 1934 – 51.

Winton, John R., ed. *A Dictionary of Economic Terms.* 3rd rev. ed. London: Routledge & K. Paul, 1951.

Woytinsky, W. S., and E. S. Woytinsky, eds. *World Population and Production: Trends and Outlook.* New York: Twentieth Century Fund, 1953.

Journals

American Economic Review
American Journal of Economics and Sociology
Economic Bulletin
Economic Journal
Economic News
Economic Studies
Journal of Economic Abstracts
Journal of Political Economy
Quarterly Journal of Economics
Review of Economics and Statistics
Southern Economic Journal

GEOGRAPHY
Books

American Geographical Society of New York. *Current Geographical Publications: Additions to the Research Catalogue of the American Geographical Society.* New York: American Geographical Society of New York, 1938 – date.

Cox, Edward Godfrey. *A Reference Guide to the Literature of Travel, Including Voyages, Geographical Descriptions, Adventures, Shipwrecks and Expeditions.* 3 vols. Seattle,

Wash.: Univ of Washington Press, 1935 – 49.

James, Preston E., and Clarence F. Jones, eds. *American Geography: Inventory and Prospect.* Syracuse, N.Y.: Association of American Geographers, by Syracuse Univ. Press, 1954.

Lock, C. B. Muriel. *Geography: A Reference Handbook.* New York: Shoe String Press, 1968.

Sealock, Richard B., and Pauline A. Seely. *Bibliography of Place Name Literature: United States, Canada, Alaska and Newfoundland.* Chicago: American Library Association, 1948.

Wright, John Kirtland, and Elizabeth T. Platt. *Aids to Geographical Research: Bibliographies, Periodicals, Atlases, Gazetteers and Other Reference Books.* 2nd ed. New York: Columbia Univ. Press, 1947.

Journals

Annals of the Association of American Geographers
Current Geographical Publications
Economic Geography
Geographical Review
Journal of Geography

HISTORY
Books

Adams, James Truslow, et al. *Album of American History.* Rev. ed. 7 vols. New York: Scribner's, 1945 – 61.

------------. *Dictionary of American History.* 2nd rev. ed. 6 vols. New York: Scribner's, 1942 – 63.

American Historical Association. *Guide to Historical Literature.* Ed. George F. Howe et al. New York: Macmillan, 1961.

Beers, Henry Putney. *Bibliographies in American History: Guide to Materials for Research.* Rev. ed. New York: H. W. Wilson, 1942.

Bellot, Hugh H. *American History and American Historians: A Review of Recent Contributions to the Interpretation of the History of the United States.* Norman, Okla.: Univ. of Oklahoma Press, 1952.

Bury, J. B., et al. *The Cambridge Ancient History.* 12 vols. Cambridge: Cambridge Univ. Press, 1923 – 39.

Coulter, Edith M., and Melanie Gerstenfeld. *Historical Bibliographies: A Systematic and Annotated Guide.* Berkeley, Calif.: Univ. of California Press, 1935.

Current, Richard N., T. H. Williams, and Frank Freidel. *American History: A Survey.* New York: Knopf, 1961.

Gray, Wood. *Historian's Handbook: A Key to the Study and Writing of History.* Boston: Houghton Mifflin, 1959.

Gwatkin, Henry M., et al. *The Cambridge Medieval History.* 8 vols. Cambridge: Cambridge Univ. Press, 1911 – 36.

Handlin, Oscar, et al., eds. *Harvard Guide to American History.* Cambridge, Mass.: Belknap Press of Harvard Univ. Press, 1954.

International Bibliography of Historical Sciences. New York: H. W. Wilson, 1930 – date.

Langer, William Leonard, comp. and ed. *An Encyclopedia of World History: Ancient, Medieval, and Modern.* 4th ed. Boston: Houghton Mifflin, 1968.

Morris, R. B., ed. *The Encyclopedia of American History.* Rev. and enl. ed. New York: Harper, 1961.

Nevins, Allan, and Howard Ehrmann, eds. *The University of Michigan History of the Modern World.* Ann Arbor: Univ. of Michigan, 1958 –. (In progress.)

Pargellis, Stanley, and D. J. Medley, eds. *Bibliography of British History: The Eighteenth Century, 1714 – 1789.* Oxford: Clarendon Press, 1951.

Sarton, George. *A Guide to the History of Science.* Waltham, Mass.: Chronica Botanica, 1952.

Schlesinger, Arthur M., and Dixon R. Fox, eds. *A History of American Life.* 12 vols. New York: Macmillan, 1927 – 44.

Ward, A. W., et al. *The Cambridge Modern History.* 13 vols. Cambridge: Cambridge Univ. Press, 1902 – 13.

Winsor, Justin, ed. *Narrative and Critical History of America.* 8 vols. Boston: Houghton, Mifflin, 1884 – 89.

Woodcock, Percival G., ed. *Concise Dictionary of Ancient History.* New York: Philosophical Library, 1955.

Writings on American History. Washington, D.C.: GPO, 1918 – 40.

Journals

American Historical Review
Economic History Review
English Historical Review
Hispanic American Historical Review
History
History Today
Journal of American History
Journal of Economic History
Journal of Modern History
Journal of Southern History
Journal of the History of Ideas
Past and Present

Renaissance News
Social Studies
Speculum

POLITICAL SCIENCE

Books

Adams, T. R. *Elements of Government: An Introduction to Political Science.* New York: Random House, 1960.

Beer, Samuel H., and Adam B. Ulam. *Patterns of Government: The Major Political Systems of Europe.* 2nd ed. New York: Random House, 1962.

Burchfield, Laverne. *Student's Guide to Materials in Political Science.* New York: Holt, 1935.

Documents on American Foreign Relations. New York: Council on Foreign Relations, 1939–date.

Dunner, Joseph, ed. *Dictionary of Political Science.* New York: Philosophical Library, 1964.

Hitchner, Dell Gillette, and William H. Harbold. *Modern Government: A Survey of Political Science.* 2nd ed. New York: Dodd, Mead, 1965.

International Bibliography of Political Science. Chicago: Aldine, 1954–date.

McLaughlin, Andrew C., and Albert B. Hart, eds. *Cyclopedia of American Government.* 3 vols. 1914; rpt. New York: Peter Smith, 1949.

Palgrave, Sir Robert Harry Inglis. *Palgrave's Dictionary of Political Economy.* Ed. Henry Higgs. 3 vols. London: Macmillan, 1925–26.

Plano, Jack C., and Milton Greenberg. *The American Political Dictionary.* New York: Holt, Rinehart and Winston, 1962.

Political Handbook and Atlas of the World. New York: Harper & Row, 1927–date.

Smith, Edward C., and Arnold J. Zurcher, eds. *Dictionary of American Politics.* Rev. ed. New York: Barnes & Noble, 1955.

Sperber, Hans. *American Political Terms: An Historical Dictionary.* Detroit: Wayne Univ. Press, 1962.

Statesman's Year-Book. London: Macmillan, 1864–date.

Theimer, Walter. *An Encylopedia of Modern World Politics.* New York: Rinehart, 1950.

Tompkins, Dorothy C. *Materials for the Study of Federal Government.* Chicago: Public Administration Service, 1948.

United Nations Yearbook. New York: Columbia Univ. Press, 1947–date.

U.S. Congress. *Biographical Directory of the*

American Congress, 1724–1961. Washington, D.C.: GPO, 1961.

The Year Book of World Affairs. London: Stevens, 1947–date.

Journals

American Political Science Review
Annals of the American Academy of Political and Social Science
Congressional Digest
Congressional Quarterly Almanac
Congressional Quarterly Weekly Report
Congressional Record
Current History
Foreign Affairs
Journal of Conflict Resolution
Journal of Politics
Midwest Journal of Political Science
Political Science Quarterly
Public Administration Review
Public Opinion Quarterly
Western Political Quarterly
World Politics

SOCIOLOGY

Books

Andriot, John L. *Guide to U.S. Government Statistics.* Arlington, Va.: Documents Index, 1961.

Current Sociological Research. New York: American Sociological Association, 1953–date.

Encyclopedia of Social Work. New York: National Association of Social Workers, 1965–date.
    Successor to *Social Work Yearbook.*

Fairchild, Henry Pratt, ed. *Dictionary of Sociology.* New York: Philosophical Library, 1944.

International Bibliography of Sociology. Chicago: Aldine, 1952–date.

Reuter, Edward B. *Handbook of Sociology.* New York: Dryden Press, 1941.

Sociological Abstracts. New York: Sociological Abstracts, 1952–date.

Journals

American Journal of Sociology
American Sociological Review
British Journal of Sociology
Human Organization
International Social Science Journal
Journal of Educational Sociology
Journal of Marriage and the Family
Social Education
Social Science

Social Science Abstracts
Social Science Review
Sociological Quarterly
Sociology and Social Research
Sociology of Education

Speech and Drama

Books

Aaronson, Charles S. *International Television Almanac.* New York: Quigley, 1956–date.

Adelman, Irving, and Rita Dworkin. *Modern Drama: A Checklist of Critical Literature on 20th Century Plays.* Metuchen, N.J.: Scarecrow Press, 1967.

American Educational Theatre Association. *A Bibliography of Theatre Arts Publications in English, 1963.* Ed. Bernard F. Dukore. Evanston, Ill.: American Educational Theatre Association, 1965.

------------. *A Selected Bibliography and Critical Comment on the Art, Theory, and Technique of Acting.* Ann Arbor, Mich.: American Educational Theatre Association, 1948.

Baker, Blanch M., comp. *Dramatic Bibliography: An Annotated List of Books on the History and Criticism of the Drama and Stage and on the Allied Arts of the Theatre.* New York: H. W. Wilson, 1933.

------------. *Theatre and Allied Arts: A Guide to Books Dealing with the History, Criticism, and Technic of the Drama and Theatre, and Related Arts and Crafts.* New York: H. W. Wilson, 1952.

Belknap, Sara. *Guide to Dance Periodicals, 1931–date.* New York: Scarecrow Press, 1950–date.

------------. *Guide to the Performing Arts, 1957–.* New York: Scarecrow Press, 1960–date.

Blum, Eleanor. *Reference Books in the Mass Media: An Annotated, Selected Booklist Covering Book Publishing, Broadcasting, Films, Newspapers, Magazines, and Advertising.* Urbana, Ill.: Univ. of Illinois Press, 1962.

Brigance, William Norwood, ed. *A History and Criticism of American Public Address.* 1943; rpt. New York: Russell & Russell, 1960.

Broderick, Gertrude G., and Patricia

Beall Hamill. *Radio and Television: A Selected Bibliography.* Washington, D.C.: U.S. Dept. of Health, Education, and Welfare, 1960.

Chujoy, Anatole, and P. W. Manchester, comps. and eds. *The Dance Encyclopedia.* Rev. and enl. ed. New York: Simon and Schuster, 1967.

Cohen, Selma J., ed. *Dictionary of Modern Ballet.* New York: Tudor, 1959.

Cornyn, Stan. *Theatre Magazine (Indexes): A Selective Index to Theatre Magazine.* New York: Scarecrow Press, 1964.

Cumulated Dramatic Index, 1909–1949: A Cumulation of the F. W. Faxon Company's Dramatic Index. 2 vols. Boston: G. K. Hall, 1965.

Duker, Sam. *Listening Bibliography.* 2nd ed. Metuchen, N.J.: Scarecrow Press, 1968.

Ewen, David. *Complete Book of the American Musical Theater: A Guide to More Than 300 Productions . . . From 1866 to the Present. . . .* New York: Holt, 1958.

------------. *Encyclopedia of the Opera.* New enl. ed. New York: Hill & Wang, 1963.

Fidell, Estelle A., and D. M. Peake, eds. *Play Index, 1949–1952; 1953–1960: An Index to 4592 Plays in 1735 Volumes.* 2 vols. New York: H. W. Wilson, 1953–63.

Firkins, Ina T. E., comp. *Index of Plays, 1800–1926.* 2 vols. New York: H. W. Wilson, 1927. Supplement, 1935.

Fulton, A. R. *Motion Pictures: The Development of an Art from Silent Films to the Age of Television.* Norman, Okla.: Univ. of Oklahoma Press, 1960.

Golter, Bob J. *Bibliography of Theses and Dissertations Relating to Audio-Visuals and Broadcasting.* Nashville: Methodist Publishing House, 1958.

Haberman, Frederick W., and James W. Cleary, comps. *Rhetoric and Public Address: A Bibliography: 1947–1961.* Madison, Wisc.: Univ. of Wisconsin Press, 1964. Continued annually in *Speech Monographs.*

Harbage, Alfred. *Annals of English Drama, 975–1700: An Analytical Record of All Plays, Extant or Lost, Chronologically Arranged and Indexed by Authors, Titles, Dramatic Companies, Etc.* Rev. S. Schoenbaum. London: Methuen, 1964.

Hare, A. Paul. *Handbook of Small Group Research.* New York: Free Press of Glencoe, 1962.

Hartnoll, Phyllis, ed. *The Oxford Companion to the Theatre.* 3rd ed. London: Oxford Univ. Press, 1967.

Hiler, Hilaire, and Meyer Hiler, comps. *Bibliography of Costume: A Dictionary Catalog of About Eight Thousand Books and Periodicals.* Ed. Helen Grant Cushing and Adah V. Morris. New York: H. W. Wilson, 1939.

Hochmuth, Marie K., ed. *A History and Criticism of American Public Address.* New York: Longmans, Green, 1955.

International Federation of Library Associations. *Performing Arts Collections: An International Handbook.* Paris: Centre National de la Recherche Scientifique, 1960.

Logasa, Hanna, and Winifred Ver Nooy, comps. *An Index to One-Act Plays, 1900– 1924.* Boston: Faxon, 1924. Supplements, 1932–date.

Loewenberg, Alfred, comp. *The Theatre of the British Isles, Excluding London: A Bibliography.* London: Society for Theatre Research, 1950.

Mulgrave, Dorothy, et al. *Bibliography of Speech and Allied Areas, 1950–1960.* Philadelphia: Chilton, 1962.

Nicoll, Allardyce. *A History of English Drama, 1660–1900.* Rev. ed. 6 vols. Cambridge: Cambridge Univ. Press, 1952–59.

Ottemiller, John H. *Index to Plays in Collections: An Author and Title Index to Plays Appearing in Collections Published Between 1900 and 1962.* 4th ed. New York: Scarecrow Press, 1964.

Palmer, Helen H., and Anne Jane Dyson. *American Drama Criticism.* New York: Shoe String Press, 1967.

------------. *European Drama Criticism.* New York: Shoe String Press, 1968.

Raffe, W. G., and M. E. Purdon. *The Dictionary of the Dance.* New York: Barnes, 1964.

Rose, Oscar. *Radio Broadcasting and Television.* New York: H. W. Wilson, 1947.

Salem, James M. *A Guide to Critical Reviews.* New York: Scarecrow Press, 1966.

Shipley, J. T. *Guide to Great Plays.* Washington, D.C.: Public Affairs Press, 1956.

Siepmann, Charles Arthur. *Television and Education in the United States.* Paris: UNESCO, 1952.

Smith, Bruce L., and Chitra M. Smith. *International Communication and Political Opinion: A Guide to the Literature.* Princeton, N.J.: Princeton Univ. Press, 1956.

------------, Harold D. Laswell, and Ralph D. Casey. *Propaganda, Communication, and Public Opinion: A Comprehensive Reference Guide.* Princeton, N.J.: Princeton Univ. Press, 1946.

Sobel, Bernard. *The Theater Handbook and Digest of Plays.* New York: Crown, 1948.

Stratman, Carl J. *Bibliography of Medieval Drama.* Berkeley, Calif.: Univ. of California Press, 1954.

Summers, Montague. *A Bibliography of the Restoration Drama.* London: Fortune Press, 1934.

Sutton, Roberta Briggs. *Speech Index.* New York: H. W. Wilson, 1935. Supplements, 1956, 1962.

Thonssen, Lester, and Elizabeth Fatherson. *Bibliography of Speech Education.* New York: H. W. Wilson, 1939. Supplement, 1950.

Van Lennep, William, et al. *The London Stage, 1660–1800: A Calendar of Plays, Entertainments & Afterpieces, Together With Casts, Box-Receipts and Contemporary Comment. Compiled from the Playbills, Newspapers and Theatrical Diaries of the Period.* 3 vols. Carbondale, Ill.: Southern Illinois Univ. Press, 1960–62.

Wallace, Karl R., ed. *History of Speech Education in America.* New York: Appleton, 1954.

West, Dorothy Herbert, and Dorothy Margaret Peake, comps. *Play Index, 1949– 1952: An Index to 2616 Plays in 1138 Volumes.* New York: H. W. Wilson, 1953.

W.P.A. Writers' Program, comp. *The Film Index: A Bibliography.* New York: Museum of Modern Art Film Library, 1941.

Zettl, Herbert. *Television Production Handbook.* San Francisco: Wadsworth, 1961.

Journals

Audio-Visual Communication Review (A-V Communication Rev.)
Business Screen (Bsns. Screen)
Educational Theatre Journal (Ed. Theatre J.)
Film News (Film N.)
Film Quarterly (Film Q.)
Modern Drama (Mod. Drama)
New York Guide and Theatre Magazine (NY Guide & Theatre Mag.)
New York Theatre Critics' Reviews (NY Theatre Critics' Rev.)
Quarterly Journal of Speech (Q. J. Speech)
Radio and Television News (Radio & TV N.)
Speech Monographs (Speech Mon.)
The Speech Teacher (Speech Teach.)
Studies in Public Communication (Stud. Public Communication)
Television Magazine (TV Mag.)
Television Quarterly (TV Q.)
Theatre
Theatre Arts
Theatre Arts Monthly
Tulane Drama Review (Tulane Drama R.)

INDEX